Published in Canada by General Publishing
Company, Ltd., 30 Lesmill Road, Don Mills,
Toronto, Ontario.
Published in the United Kingdom by Con-
stable and Company, Ltd., 10 Orange Street,
London WC2H 7EG.

International Standard Book Number:
0-486-20802-8
Library of Congress Catalog Card Number:
75-5012

Manufactured in the United States of America
Dover Publications, Inc.
180 Varick Street
New York, N.Y. 10014

DÍGALO EN INGLÉS
PARA LOS DE HABLA ESPAÑOLA

Say It In English
for Spanish-speaking People

BY
LEON J. COHEN
Goshen Central School
Goshen, N.Y.
and
A. C. ROGERS

NEW YORK
DOVER PUBLICATIONS, INC.

TABLA DE MATERIAS

En esta edición mejorada de este libro, se observa que faltan unos números entre las secciones. Esto no significa que hay omisiones en el texto.

SISTEMA DE PRONUNCIACIÓN

En inglés las vocales tienen varios sonidos según la palabra en donde se encuentran y son diptongos más bien que sonidos puros. Además, se dividen las palabras en sílabas de un modo diferente.

Se debe leer la pronunciación indicada en estas páginas como palabras españolas, con el acento tónico en la sílaba en letra mayúscula y los sonidos de acuerdo con esta clave:
Siempre

a—como *a* en *casa*

aa—más breve que la *a* en *balcón*

b—como *b* en *hombre*

d—como *d* en *mendigo*

dch—como *dch* en *decid chistes*

e—como *e* en *del*

g—como *g* en *gato* y nunca como la *g* en *gente*

î—más abierta y breve que la *i* en *mil*

o—como *o* en *no entre*

r—como *r* en *cura* pero más débil

s—como *s* en *suma*

ŝ—como *s* en *mismo*

sh—como la *ch* francesa en *chapeau* y *chef*, la *sch* alemana en *fisch* o la *sc* italiana en *pesce*

5

th—como *d* en *lado* pero más fuerte

û—más abierta y breve que la *u* en *cubo* y como la *e* francesa en *le*

v—como *v* en *lavar*, casi una *f* sonora

z—como la *z* castellana en *luz* y *zapato*

El mejor método de aprender a hablar inglés es imitar los sonidos al oírlos en el disco y en el habla de los norteamericanos.

EXPRESIONES UTILES
USEFUL EXPRESSIONS

1. Sí. No. Puede ser.
Yes. No. Perhaps.
yes. no. pûr-HAAPS.

2. Haga el favor de ——. Dispénseme.
Please ——. Excuse me.
plis ——. ecs-QUIÛS mi.

3. (Muchas) gracias.
Thanks (very much).
zaancs (VER-y múch).

4. No hay de que.
You are welcome.
yu ar HUEL-cûm.

5. ¿Habla usted alemán (español, italiano)?
Do you speak German (Spanish, Italian)?
du yu spic DCHÛR-mún, (SPAAN-ish, i-TAL-yûn)?

6. Sólo hablo inglés (francés, español).
I speak only English (French, Spanish).
ay spic ON-li ÎNG-lish, (french, SPAAN-ish).

7. Alemán, italiano.
German, Italian.
DCHÛR-mún, i-TAL-yún.

8. Soy de ——.
   I am from ——.
   ay aam frûm ——.

9. Mi dirección (para cartas) es ——.
   My (mailing) address is ——.
   may (MEIL-îng) aa-DRES îŝ ——.

10. Él (Ella) es de ——.
   He (She) is from ——.
   ji (shi) îŝ frûm ——.

11. Favor de hablar (más) despacio.
   Please speak (more) slowly.
   pliŝ spic (mor) SLOU-li.

12. (No) comprendo.
   I (do not) understand.
   ay (du nat) ûn-dûr-STAAND.

13. Favor de repetirlo.
   Repeat it, please.
   ri-PIT ît, pliŝ.

14. Otra vez.   También.
   Again.   Also.
   û-GUEN, OL-sou.

15. Escríbalo, por favor.
   Write it down, please.
   rait ît daun, pliŝ.

16. ¿ Qué desea usted ?
   What do you wish ?
   huat du yu huîsh ?

17. ¿ Cuánto es ?
How much is it?
jau mûch îŝ ît?

18. Venga acá.   Pase usted.
Come here.   Come in.
cûm jir.   cûm în.

19. Espere un momento.
Wait a moment.
hueit û MOU-ment.

20. ¿ Por qué ?   ¿ Cuándo ?
Why?   When?
huay?   huen?

21. ¿ Cómo ?   ¿ Cuánto tiempo ?
How?   How long?
jau?   jau long?

22. ¿ A qué distancia ?   ¿ Quién ?   ¿ Qué ?
How far?   Who?   What?
jau far?   ju?   huat?

23. ¿Dónde está (están) —— ?
Where is (are) —— ?
huer îŝ (ar) —— ?

24. Caballeros o Señores.   Damas o Señoras.
The Men's Room.   The Ladies' Room.
thû menŝ rum.   thû LEI-diŝ rum.

25. Aquí, allí.
Here, there.
jir, ther.

26. (No) está bien.
It is (not) all right.
ît îŝ (nat) ol rait.

27. Es viejo (nuevo).
It is old (new).
ît îŝ ould (niu).

28. Vacío, lleno.
Empty, full.
EMP-ti, fûl.

29. Eso (no) es todo.
That is (not) all.
thaat îŝ (nat) ol.

30. A, de, con.
To, from, with.
tu, frûm, huîth.

31. En, sobre, cerca de, lejos de.
In, on, near, far.
în, an, nir, far.

32. Enfrente de, detrás de.
In front of, behind.
în frûnt ûv, bi-JAIND.

33. Al lado de, dentro de, fuera de.
Beside, inside, outside.
bi-SAID, ÎN-said, AUT-said.

34. Algo, nada.
Something, nothing.
SÛM-zíng, NÛZ-îng.

35. Unos. Pocos.
Several. Few.
SEV-rúl. fiu.

36. (Mucho) más, menos.
(Much) more, less.
(mûch) mor, les.

37. (Un poco) más, menos.
(A little) more, less.
(û LÎT-úl) mor, les.

38. Suficiente, demasiado.
Enough, too much.
i-NÛF, tu mûch.

39. Mucho, muchos.
Much, many.
mûch, MEN-y.

40. Bueno, mejor (que).
Good, better (than).
gûd, BET-ûr (thaan).

41. Mal, peor (que).
Bad, worse (than).
baad, wûrs (thaan).

42. Ahora, en seguida.
Now, immediately.
nau, î-MID-i-ût-li.

43. Pronto, más tarde.
Soon, later.
sun, LEI-tûr.

44. Lo más pronto posible.
As soon as possible.
aaŝ sun aaŝ PA-sî-búl.

45. A más tardar.   Por lo menos.
At the latest.   At least.
aat thû LEI-test.   aat list.

46. Es (muy) tarde.
It is (too) late.
ît îŝ (tu) leit.

47. Es temprano.
It is early.
ît îŝ ÛR-li.

48. Despacio, más despacio.
Slow, slower.
slou, SLOU-ûr.

49. Aprisa, más aprisa.
Quickly, faster.
CUÎC-li, FAAS-tûr.

50. (No) tengo prisa.
I am (not) in a hurry.
ay aam (nat) ín û JÛR-y.

51. Tengo calor (frío).
I am warm (cold).
ay aam huorm (could).

52. Tengo (hambre, sed, sueño).
I am (hungry, thirsty, sleepy).
ay aam (JÛN-gri, ZÛRS-ti, SLIP-y).

53. Estoy (ocupado, cansado, enfermo, extraviado).

I am (busy, tired, ill, lost).

ay aam (BÍS-y, taird, íl, lost).

54. ¿ Qué pasa aquí ?

What is the matter here?

huat îs thû MAAT-ûr jir?

55. ¡Socorro! ¡Fuego! ¡Ladrón!

Help! Fire! Thief!

jelp! FAI-ûr! zif!

56. ¡ Cuidado !

Look out!

lûc aut!

57. ¡Oiga! ¡Mire!

Listen! Look here!

LÍS-ûn! lûc jir!

58. ¿ Puede usted (ayudarme, decirme) ?

Can you (help me, tell me)?

caan yu (jelp mi, tel mi)?

59. Busco ——.

I am looking for ——.

ay aam LÛ-quing for ——.

60. Quisiera ——.

I should like ——.

ay shûd laic ——.

61. ¿ Puede usted recomendar (un buen) ——?

Can you recommend (a good)——?

caan vu rec- û-MEND (û gûd)——?

62. Me alegro.   Lo siento.
I am glad.   I am sorry.
ay aam glaad.   ay aam SAR-y.

63. ¿ Desea usted ——— ?
Do you want ——— ?
du yu huant ——— ?

64. (No) es mi culpa.
It is (not) my fault.
ît îŝ (nat) may folt.

65. ¿ Quién tiene la culpa ?
Whose fault is it?
juŝ folt îŝ ît ?

66. (No) sé.
I (don't) know.
ay (dount) nou.

67. Creo que sí (no).
I (don't) think so.
ay (dount) zînc sou.

68. ¿ Para qué es eso ?
What is that for ?
huat îŝ thaat for ?

69. ¿ Cómo se llama esto en inglés ?
What is this called in English?
huat îŝ thîs cold in ÎNG-lîsh ?

70. ¿ Cómo se dice ——— ?
How do you say ——— ?
jau du yu sey ——— ?

71. ¿ Cómo se deletrea —— ?
How do you spell —— ?
jau du yu spel —— ?

DIFICULTADES
DIFFICULTIES

74. No puedo hallar la dirección de mi hotel.
I can't find my hotel address.
ay caant faind may jou-TEL aa-DRES.

75. No recuerdo el nombre de la calle.
I don't remember the street.
ay dount ri-MEM-bûr thû strit.

76. No encuentro a mis amigos.
I have lost my friends.
ay jaav lost may frendŝ.

77. Dejé mi (bolsa, cartera) en ——.
I left my (purse, wallet) in the ——.
ay left may (pûrs, HUAL-ît) in thû ——.

78. Olvidé (mi dinero, mis llaves).
I forgot (my money, my keys).
ay for-GAT (may MÛN-y, may quiŝ).

79. He perdido mi (tren, avión, autobús).
I have missed my (train, plane, bus).
ay jaav mîst may (trein, plein, bûs).

80. ¿Qué debo hacer ?
What am I to do?
huat aam ay tu du?

81. Usted dijo que costaría ——.
You said it would cost ——.
yu sed ít U-úd cost ——.

82. Váyase.   Go away.   *gou ú-HUEY.*

83. Ellos (nos, me) molestan.
They are bothering (us, me).
they ar BATH-úr-íng (ús, mi).

84. Llamaré un policía.
I will call a policeman.
ay huíl col ú po-LIS-mún.

85. ¿ Dónde está la jefatura de policía ?
Where is the police station?
huer ís thú po-LIS STEI-shún?

86. Me han robado el bolsillo.
I have been robbed of my purse.
ay jaav bín rabd úv may púrs.

87. La sección de objetos perdidos.
The Lost and Found Desk.
thú lost aand faund desc.

SALUDOS Y PRESENTACIONES
GREETINGS AND INTRODUCTIONS

90. Buenos días, buenas noches.
Good morning, good evening.
gúd MOR-níng, gúd IV-níng.

91. Aló, adiós.
Hello, good-bye.
jel-OU, gúd-BAY.

92. Hasta la vista.
I'll be seeing you.
ail bi SI-ing yu.

93. Me llamo ——.
My name is ——.
may neim îs ——.

94. ¿ Cómo se llama ?
What is your name?
huat îs yur neim?

95. ¿ Permítame presentar al señor——, a la señora ——, a la señorita —— ?
May I introduce Mr. ——, Mrs. ——, Miss —— ?
may ay ín-tro-DUS MÎS-túr ——, MÎS-îs ——, 'mîs ——?

96. Mi esposa, mi esposo.
My wife, my husband.
may huaif, may JÚS-búnd.

97. Mi hija, mi hijo.
My daughter, my son.
may DOT-úr, may sún.

98. Mi amigo. My friend. *may frend.*

99. Mi hermana, mi hermano.
My sister, my brother.
may SÎS-túr, may BRÚTH-úr.

100. Tanto gusto. How do you do.
jau du yu du.

101. ¿ Cómo está usted ? How are you?
jau ar yu?

102. Bien, y ¿usted?   Fine, and you?
fain, aand yu?

103. ¿ Cómo está su familia ?
How is your family?
jau îŝ yur FAAM-î-li?

104. (No) muy bien.
(Not) very well.
(nat) VER-y huel.

105. Haga el favor de sentarse.
Please sit down.   *plîŝ sît daun.*

106. Me he divertido mucho.
I have enjoyed myself very much.
ay jaav end-CHOID mai-SELF VER-y mûch.

107. Espero verle (otra vez, pronto).
I hope to see you (again, soon).
ay joup tu si yu (û-GUEN, sun).

108. Venga usted a verme.
Come to see me.   *cûm tu si mi.*

**109. Déme su dirección (y su número de
teléfono).**
Give me your address (and telephone
number).
*gív mi yur aa-DRES (aand TEL-û-foun
NÛM-búr).*

110. Dé mis recuerdos a ——.
Give my regards to ——.
guív may ri-GARDŜ tu ——.

III. Viajamos a ——.
We are traveling to ——.
huy ar TRAAV-úl-ing tu ——.

VIAJES: EXPRESIONES GENERALES
TRAVEL: GENERAL EXPRESSIONS

114. Quiero ir a la oficina de la línea aérea.
I want to go to the air line office.
ay huant tu gou tu thi er lain OF-ís.

115. El aeropuerto.   La estación de autobuses.
The airport.   The bus station.
thi ER-port.   thú bús STEI-shún.

116. El muelle.   La estación de ferrocarriles.
The dock.   The railroad station.
thú dac.   thú REIL-roud STEI-shún.

117. ¿ En cuánto tiempo se llega a —— ?
How long will it take to go to —— ?
jau long huíl ít teic tu gou tu —— ?

118. ¿ Cuándo llegaremos a —— ?
When will we arrive at —— ?
huen huíl huy ú-RAIV aat —— ?

119. Haga el favor de llamarme un taxi.
Please get me a taxi.
plíś guet mi ú TAAC-si.

120. La taquilla.   The ticket office.
thú TÍ-quít OF-ís.

121. Un billete, un horario.
　　A ticket, a timetable.
　　û TÍ-quit, û TAIM-tei-bûl.

122. Un mozo.　La sala de equipajes.
　　A porter.　The baggage room.
　　û POR-tûr.　thû BAAG-îdch rum.

123. El andén.　The platform.
　　thû PLAAT-form.

124. ¿ Está reservado este asiento ?
　　Is this seat taken?
　　îŝ thîs sit TEI-quen?

125. ¿ Pudeo reservar un asiento (delan-tero) ?
　　Can I reserve a (front) seat?
　　caan ay ri-ŜÛRV û (frûnt) sit ?

126. Un asiento cerca de la ventana.
　　A seat near the window.
　　û sit nir thû HUÎN-dou.

127. ¿ Es éste el camino directo a —— ?
　　Is this the direct way to —— ?
　　îŝ thîs thû dai-RECT huey tu —— ?

128. ¿ Cómo se va (allá) ?
　　How does one go (there)?
　　jau dûŝ huon gou (ther) ?

129. ¿ Dónde doy vuelta ?
　　Where do I turn?
　　huer du ay tûrn?

130. Al norte, al sur.
To the north, to the south.
tu thû norz, tu thû sauz.

131. Al oeste, al este.
To the west, to the east.
tu thû huest, tu thi ist.

132. A la derecha, a la izquierda.
To the right, to the left.
tu thû rait, tu thû left.

133. Adelante.   Straight ahead.
streit û-JED.

134. Adelante, atrás.   Forward, back.
FOR-u-hûrd, baac.

135. Calle, círculo, plaza.
Street, circle, square *o* place.
strit, SÛR-cûl, scuer, pleis.

136. ¿ Me encamino correctamente ?
Am I going in the right direction ?
aam ay GOU-îng în thû rait dî-REC-shún ?

137. ¿ Tengo que cambiar ?
Do I have to change ?
du ay jaav tu cheindch ?

138. Por favor, avíseme dónde me bajo.
Please tell me where to get off.
pliŝ tel mi huer tu guet of.

ADUANA
AT THE CUSTOMS

141. Éste es mi equipaje, —— piezas.
This is my baggage, —— pieces.
thîs îŝ may BAAG-îdch, —— PI-sîŝ.

142. Aquí tiene usted mi (pasaporte, permiso).
Here is my (passport, permit).
jir îŝ may (PAAS-port, PÛR-mît).

143. ¿ Debo abrir todo ?
Shall I open everything?
shaal ay OU-pen EV-ri-zîng?

144. No puedo abrir ése.
I cannot open that.
ay CAAN-nat OU-pen thaat.

145. Perdí mi llave.   I have lost my key.
ay jaav lost may qui.

146. No tengo nada que declarar.
I have nothing to declare.
ay haav NÛZ-îng tu di-CLER.

147. Todo esto es para mi uso personal.
All this is for my personal use.
ol thîs îŝ for may PÛR-sú-nûl yus.

148. No hay más que —— aquí.
There is nothing here but ——.
ther îŝ NÛZ-îng jir bût ——.

149. Éstos son regalos.   These are gifts.
thîs ar guífts.

150. **¿ Hay que pagar impuestos sobre estos artículos ?**
Are these things dutiable?
ar this zíngs DIU-ti-û-búl ?

151. **¿ Cuánto tengo que pagar ?**
How much must I pay?
jau mûch mûst ay pey?

152. Esto es todo lo que tengo.
This is all I have.
this îs ol ay jaav.

153. Haga el favor de tener cuidado.
Please be careful.
plis bi QUER-fúl.

154. ¿ Ha terminado usted ?
Have you finished?
jaav yu FÎN-íshɩ?

155. Se me perdió el equipaje.
I cannot find my baggage.
ay CAAN-nat faind may BAAG-îdch.

156. Mi tren sale en —— minutos.
My train leaves in —— minutes.
may trein livs în ——MÎN-îts.

BILLETES
TICKETS

159. ¿ Cuánto cuesta un billete a —— ?
How much is a ticket to —— ?
jau mûch îs û TÎ-quît tu —— ?

160. Un billete sencillo (de ida y vuelta).
   One-way(round trip)ticket.
   HUON-huey (raund trîp) TÎ-quit.

161. Pullman, coche.   Pullman, coach.
   PÛL-mún, couch.

162. Cama (alta, baja).   Compartimiento.
   (Upper, lower) berth.   Roomette.
   (Û-pûr, LOU-ûr) bûrz.   ru-MET.

163. ¿ Puedo ir vía —— ?
   Can I go by way of —— ?
   caan ay gou bay huey úv —— ?

164. ¿ Por cuántos días es bueno este billete ?
   How long is this ticket good ?
   jau long îs thîs TÎ-quit gûd ?

165. ¿ Cuántos kilos de equipaje se permiten llevar ?
   How much baggage may I take ?
   jau mûch BAAG-idch may ay teic ?

166. ¿ Se puede comer en camino ?
   Can I get something to eat on the way ?
   caan ay guet SÛM-zîng tu it an thû huey ?

167. ¿ Cuánto por libra de exceso ?
   How much per pound for excess ?
   jau mûch pûr paund for EC-ses ?

168. ¿ Hay seguro para viajeros ?
   Is there travel insurance ?
   îs ther TRAAV-ûl în-SHUR-úns ?

EQUIPAJE
BAGGAGE

169. ¿ Dónde se factura el equipaje ?
Where is the baggage checked ?
huer îŝ thû BAAG-îdch chect?

170. Quiero dejar estas maletas un rato.
I want to leave these bags for a while.
ay huant tu liv thîŝ baagŝ for û huail.

171. ¿ Debo pagar ahora o después ?
Do I pay now or later?
du ay pey nau or LEI-tûr ?

172. Quiero reclamar mi equipaje.
I want to take out my baggage.
ay huant tu teic aut may BAAG-îdch,

173. Aquél es el mío.   That is mine there.
thaat îŝ main ther.

174. Mucho cuidado con esto.
Handle this very carefully.
JAAN-dûl thîs VER-y QUER-fûl-y.

TREN
TRAIN

175. Voy en tren a ——.
I am going by train to ——.
ay aam GOU-îng bay trein tu ——.

176. ¿ Está a la hora el tren para —— ?
Is the train for —— on time?
îŝ thû trein for —— an taim?

177. Está retrasado de —— minutos.
It is —— minutes late.
it ís —— MÍN-íts leit.

178. Hágame el favor de poner esto en la reja.
Please put this in the rack.
plíš pût thís ín thû raac.

179. Favor de cerrar (abrir) la ventanilla.
Please open (close) the window.
plíš OU-pen (clouš) thû HUÍN-dou.

180. ¿Dónde está el comedor (carro fumador)?
Where is the diner (smoker)?
huer íš thû DAIN-ûr (SMOUC-ûr)?

181. ¿Le molesta que fume?
Do you mind my smoking?
du yu maind may SMOU-quíng?

182. ¿A qué hora sirven el desayuno (almuerzo, comida)?
What time is breakfast (lunch, dinner)?
huat taim íš BREC-fûst (lûnch, DÍN-ûr)?

AVIÓN
AIRPLANE

185. ¿Hay servicio de transporte al aeropuerto?
Is there motor service to the airport?
íš ther MOU-tûr SÛR-vís tu thi ER-port?

186. ¿ A qué hora vienen por mí ?
At what time will they come for me?
aat huat taim huíl they cûm for mi?

187. ¿ A qué hora sale el avión para —— ?
When is there a plane to —— ?
huen îŝ ther û plein tu —— ?

188. ¿ Se sirven comidas en el avión ?
Is food served on the plane?
îŝ fud sûrvd an thû plein?

189. ¿ Cuántas libras puedo llevar ?
How may pounds may I take?
jau MEN-y paundŝ mey ay teic?

AUTOBÚS
BUS

192. ¿ Con qué frecuencia salen los omni-buses a —— ?
How often do buses go to —— ?
jau OF-ún du BÚS-îŝ gou tu —— ?

193. ¿ Puedo comprar un billete de excursión ?
Can I buy an excursion ticket?
caan ay bay aan ecs-CÛR-shún TÍ-quît?

194. ¿ Paran para comer ?
Is there a stop for lunch?
îŝ ther û stap for lúnch?

195. ¿ Puedo hacer escala por la noche ?
Can I stop overnight on the way?
caan ay stap ou-vûr-NAIT an thû huey?

BARCO
BOAT

198. ¿ Puedo ir por vapor a —— ?
Can I go by boat to ——?
caan ay gou bay bout tu ——?

199. ¿ Cuándo sale el próximo barco ?
When does .the next boat leave?
huen dûŝ thû necst bout liv?

200. ¿ A qué hora debo embarcarme ?
When must I go on board?
huen mûst ay gou an bourd?

201. ¿ Puedo desembarcar en —— ?
Can.I land at ——?
caan ay laand aat ——?

202. ¿ Se sirven comidas a bordo ?
Are meals served on board?
ar milŝ sûrvd an bourd?

203. El capitán, el contador.
The captain, the purser.
thû CAAP-tín, thû PÛR-sûr.

204. El camerero, la cubierta.
The steward, the deck.
thû STU-hûrd, thû dec.

205. Quiero alquilar una silla.
I want to rent a deck chair.
ay huant tu rent û dec cher.

206. Estoy mareado.
I am seasick.
ay aam SI-síc.

207. Voy a mi camarote.
I am going to my cabin.
ay aam GOU-îng tu may CAA-bîn.

208. Vamos al comedor (bar).
Let's go to the dining room (bar).
lets gou tu thû DAIN-îng rum (bar).

209. Una lancha, un salvavidas.
A lifeboat, a life preserver.
û LAIF-bout, û laif pri-ŜÛR-vûr.

AUTOMÓVIL Y TURISMO
AUTOMOBILE AND MOTORING

212. ¿ Dónde hay un (expendio de gasolina, garaje) ?
Where is there a (gas station, garage)?
huer îŝ ther û (gaas STEI-shûn, gû-RADCH) ?

213. ¿ Es un buen camino ?
Is the road good?
îŝ thû roud gûd.

214. ¿ Está pavimentado o es de tierra ?
Is it hard or dirt surface?
îŝ ît jard or dûrt SÛR-fîŝ?

215. ¿ Cómo se llama este pueblo (el próximo) ?
What town is this (the next one)?
huat taun îŝ thîs (thû necst huon) ?

216. ¿ Adónde conduce aquel camino ?
Where does that road go?
huer dûŝ thaat roud gou?

217. Información para turistas.
The tourist club.
thû TU-rîst clûb.

218. Tengo una licencia automovilista internacional.
I have an international driver's license.
ay jaav aan în-tûr-NAASH-û-nûl DRAI-vûrŝ LAI-sens.

219. Quiero aire.   I want some air.
ay huant sûm er.

220. ¿Cuánto cuesta la gasolina por galón?
How much is gas a gallon?
jau mûch îŝ gaas û GAAL-ûn?

221. Déme —— galones.
Give me —— gallons.
guîv mi —— GAAL-ûns.

222. Por favor, cambie el aceite.
Please change the oil.
pliŝ cheindch thi oil.

223. Aceite (delgado, mediano, grueso).
(Light, medium, heavy) oil.
(lait, MI-di-ûm, JEV-y) oil.

224. Ponga agua en el radiador.
Put water in the radiator.
pût HUOT-ûr în thû REI-di-ei-tûr.

225. ¿Quiere engrasar el coche?
Will you lubricate the car?
huîl yu LU-brî-qteit thû car?

226. ¿ Podría lavarlo (ahora, pronto) ?
Could you wash it (now, soon) ?
cûd yu huash ît (nau, sun) ?

227. Ajuste los frenos.
Tighten the brakes.
TAI-ten thû breics.

228.¿ Quiere usted revisar los neumáticos ?
Will you check the tires?
huîl yu chec thû TAI-ûrŝ ?

229. ¿ Puede componer la llanta pinchada ?
Can you fix the flat tire?
caan yu fîcs thû flaat TAI-ûr ?

230.¿ Qué tiene ?
What is wrong ?
huat îŝ rong ?

231. Un pinchazo, un escape.
A puncture, a slow leak.
û PÛNC-chûr, û slou lic.

232. —— no funciona (bien).
The —— does not work (well).
thû —— dûŝ nat huorc (huel).

233. Hay un (rechinamiento, ruido).
There is a (grinding, noise).
ther îŝ û (GRAIND-ing, noiŝ).

234. Hay un (golpeteo, chirrido).
There is a (rattle, squeak).
ther îŝ û (RAAT-ûl, scuic).

235. Hay un goteo.
There is a leak.
ther iŝ û lic.

236. ¿ Me permite estacionarme aquí un rato ?
May I park here for a while?
mey ay parc jir for û huail?

237. Quiero guardar mi auto por la noche.
I want to garage my car for the night.
au huant tu gû-RADCH may car for thû nait.

238. ¿ A qué hora se abre (se cierra) ?
When does it open (close) ?
huen dûŝ ît OU-pen (clouŝ) ?

AYUDA EN EL CAMINO
HELP ON THE ROAD

241. Siento mucho incomodarle.
I am sorry to trouble you.
ay aam SOR-y tu TRÛ-bûl yu.

242. Mi coche no funciona.
My car has broken down.
may car jaaŝ BROU-quen daun.

243. ¿ Puede usted remolcarme (empujarme) ?
Can you tow (push) me?
caan yu tou (pûsh) mi?

244. ¿ Puede usted ayudarme a alzar el carro con el gato ?

Can you help me jack up the car?

caan yu jelp mi dchaac ûp thû car?

245. ¿ Quiere usted ayudarme a poner la rueda de repuesto ?

Will you help me put on the spare?

huíl yu jelp mi pût an thû sper?

246. ¿ Puede usted darme un poco de gasolina ?

Could you give me some gas?

cûd yu guív mi sûm gaas?

247. ¿ Quiere usted llevarme a un garaje ?

Will you take me to a garage?

huíl yu teic mi tu û gû-RADCH?

248. ¿ Quiere usted ayudarme a apartar el coche del camino ?

Will you help get the car off the road?

huíl yu jelp guet thû car of thû roud?

249. Mi carro está atascado.

My car is stuck in the mud.

may car iŝ stûc ín thû mûd.

250. Está en la zanja.

It is in the ditch.

ît iŝ ín thû dích.

PARTES DEL CARRO
PARTS OF THE CAR

253. Acelerador.   Accelerator.

aac-SEL-û-rei-tûr.

254. Acumulador. Battery. *BAAT-ûr-y.*

255. Tornillo. Bolt. *boult.*

256. Freno. Brake. *breic.*

257. Motor. Engine. *EN-dchîn.*

258. Tuerca. Nut. *nût.*

259. Muelle. Spring. *sprîng.*

260. Arranque. Starter. *START-ûr.*

261. Volante. Steering wheel.
STIR-îng huil.

262. Faro delantero. Head light.
jed lait.

263. Foco trasero. Tail light. *teil lait.*

264. Cámara. Tube. *tub.*

265. Llanta. Tire. *TAI-ûr.*

266. Rueda (trasera, delantera, de la izquierda, de la derecha).
(Back, front, left, right) wheel.
(*baac, frûnt, left, rait*) *huîl.*

HERRAMIENTAS Y EQUIPO
TOOLS AND EQUIPMENT

269. Cadenas. Chains. *cheinŝ.*

270. Martillo. Hammer. *JAAM-ûr.*

271. Gato. Jack. *dchaac.*

272. Llave. Key. *qui.*

273. Pinzas. Pliers. *PLAI-ûrŝ.*

274. Soga. Rope. *roup.*

275. Destornillador. Screwdriver.
SCRU-draiv-ûr.

276. Bomba (de neumáticos). Tire pump.
TAI-ûr púmp.

277. Llave de tuercas. Wrench. *rench.*

LETREROS DEL CAMINO Y AVISOS
ROAD SIGNS AND PUBLIC NOTICES

280. Bulevar. Boulevard. *BUL-û-vard.*

281. Cerrado. Closed. *cloûsd.*

282. Cruce. Crossroads. *CROS-roudŝ.*

283. Curva. Curve. *cûrv.*

284. Peligro. Danger. *DEIN-dchûr.*

285. Desvío. Detour. *DI-tur.*

286. Columpio. Dip. *díp.*

287. Curva doble. Double curve.
DÛB-ûl cûrv.

288. Cuidado. Drive carefully.
draiv QUER-fúl-y.

289. Entrada. Entrance. *En-trúns.*

290. Salida. Exit. *ECS-ît.*

291. Adelante. Go. *gou.*

292. Cables de alta tensión.
High tension lines.
jay TEN-shûn lainŝ.

293. Camino lateral.   Road intersection
roud ín-tûr-SEC-shûn.

294. Prohibido el paso.   Keep out.
quip aut.

295. Conserve su derecha.   Keep right.
quip rait.

296. Damas.   Ladies.   *LEI-dis.*

297. Caballeros.   Men.   *men.*

298. Puente angosto.   Narrow bridge.
NAAR-ou brîdch.

299. Camino angosto.   Narrow road.
NAAR-ou roud.

300. Trabajadores.   Men working.
men u-ÛR-quíng.

301. Prohibido estacionarse.   No parking.
nou PAR-quíng.

302. Prohibida vuelta (a la derecha, izquierda).
No (right, left) turn.
nou (rait, left) tûrn.

303. Se prohibe fumar.   No smoking.
nou SMOU-quíng.

304. No hay paso.   No thoroughfare.
nou ZÛR-ou-fer.

305. Sentido único.   One way.   *huon huey.*

306. Estacionamiento.   Parking.
PAR-quíng.

307. Fin del pavimento. Pavement ends.
PEIV-ment endŝ.

308. F. C. (Ferrocarril).
Railroad crossing.
REIL-roud CROS-ing.

309. Camino en reparación.
Road repairs.
roud ri-PERŜ.

310. Escuela. School. *scul.*

311. Codo. Sharp turn. *sharp túrn.*

312. Modere su velocidad. Slow down.
slou daun.

313. Bajada. Steep grade. *stip greid.*

314. Parada obligatoria. Alto.
Full stop. Stop.
fúl stap. stap.

315. Pare, mire y escuche.
Stop! Look! Listen!
stap! lûc! LÎS-ún!

316. Puente provisional.
Temporary bridge.
TEM-pû-rer-y brîdch.

317. Frene con motor. Use second gear.
yuŝ SEC-únd guir.

318. Camino sinuoso. Winding road.
HUAIND-ing roud.

AUTOBÚS Y TRANVÍA
LOCAL BUS AND STREETCAR

320. La parada, el chófer.
The bus stop, the driver.
thû bûs stap, thû DRAIV-ûr.

**321. ¿ Qué autobús (tranvía) tomo para
—— ?**
What bus (car) do I take to ——?
huat bûs (car) du ay teic tu ——?

**322. ¿ Dónde para el autobús (el tranvía)
para —— ?**
Where does the bus (car) for —— stop?
huer dûŝ thû bûs (car) for —— stap?

323. ¿ Pasa usted cerca de —— ?
Do you go near ——?
du yu gou nir ——?

324. ¿ Cuánto cuesta el pasaje ?
How much is the fare?
jou much iŝ thû fer?

**325. La próxima parada. Dos paradas
más.**
The next stop. Two more stops.
thû necst stap. tu mor staps.

TAXI
TAXI

328. Haga el favor de llamarme un taxi.
Please call a taxi for me.
pliŝ col û TAAC-si for mi.

329. Quiero ir a ——.
I wish to go to ——.
ay huísh tu gou tu ——.

330. ¿ A qué distancia está ?
How far is it?
jau far îs ît?

331. ¿ Cuánto costará ?
How much will it be?
jau mûch huíl ît bi?

332. ¿ Cuánto cobra usted por hora (milla) ?
What do you charge per hour (mile)?
huat du yu chardch púr AU-ûr (mail)?

333. Eso es demasiado. That is too much.
thaat îs tu mûch.

334. Quiero solamente pasearme.
I just wish to drive around.
ay dchúst huísh tu draiv û-RAUND.

335. Por favor, conduzca (más despacio, con más cuidado).
Please drive (more slowly, more carefully).
plîs draiv (mor SLOU-li, mor QUER-fúl-y).

336. Pare aquí. Espéreme.
Stop here. Wait for me.
stap hir. hueit for mi.

337. ¿ Cuánto debo ?
How much do I owe?
jau mûch du ay hou?

ALOJAMIENTO: HOTEL
LODGING: HOTEL

340. ¿ **Qué hotel es (bueno, barato)** ?
Which hotel is (good, inexpensive) ?
huích jou-TEL îŝ (gúd, în-ecs-PEN-sîv) ?

341. El mejor hotel. The best hotel.
thû best jou-TEL.

342. No demasiado caro.
Not too expensive.
nat tu ecs-PEN-sîv.

343. (No) quiero estar en el centro.
I (do not) want to be in the center of town.
ay (du nat)huant tu bi în thû SEN-tûr ûv taun.

344. Tengo reservado ——.
I have a reservation for ——.
ay jaav û reŝ-ûr-VEI-shûn for ——.

345. Quiero hacer una reservación.
I want to make a reservation.
ay huant tu meic û reŝ-ûr-VEI-shûn.

346. Quiero un cuarto con (sin) comidas.
I want a room with (without) meals.
ay huant û rum huîth (huîth-AUT) milŝ.

347. Quiero un cuarto para uno (para dos).
I want a single (double) room.
ay huant û SÎN-gûl (DÛ-bûl) rum.

348. Una suite, una cama.
A suite, a bed.
û suit, û bed.

349. Con baño, ducha, camas gemelas.
With bath, shower, twin beds.
huîth baaz, SHAU-ûr, tuín bedŝ.

350. Con una ventana.   With a window.
huîth û HUÍN-dou.

351. Un cuarto al frente (al fondo).
A front (back) room.
û frûnt (baac) rum.

352. Por —— días.   Para esta noche.
For —— days.   For tonight.
for —— deiŝ.   for tû-NAIT.

353. Para —— personas.
For —— persons.
for —— PÛR-sûnŝ.

354. ¿ Cuánto cuesta al día ?
What is the rate per day ?
huat îŝ thû reit pûr dey ?

355. Por semana, por mes.
A week, a month.
û huic, û mûnth.

356. ¿ En qué piso ?
On what floor ?
an huat flor ?

357. Arriba, abajo.
Upstairs, downstairs.
ÛP-sterŝ, DAUN-sterŝ.

358. ¿ Hay ascensor ?
Is there an elevator ?
îŝ ther aan EL-û-vei-tûr ?

359. Agua corriente, agua caliente.
Running water, hot water.
RÚN-ing HUOT-ûr, jat HUOT-ûr.

360. Quiero un cuarto en un piso más alto.
I want a room higher up.
ay huant û rum JAI-ûr úp.

361. En un piso más bajo.
On a lower floor.
an û LOU-ûr flor.

362. Quisiera ver el cuarto.
I should like to see the room.
ay shûd laic tu si thû rum.

363. ¿Dónde está el baño (comedor)?
Where is the bathroom (dining room)?
huer îs thû BAAZ-rum (DAIN-îng rum)?

364. Éste (no) me gusta.
I (do not) like this one.
ay (du nat) laic thîs huon.

365. ¿Tiene usted uno mejor?
Have you something better?
jaav yu SÛM-zîng BET-ûr?

366. Más barato, más grande, más pequeño.
Cheaper, larger, smaller.
CHIP-ûr, LARD-chûr, SMOL-ûr.

367. Con más luz (más ventilación).
With more light (more air).
huîth mor lait (mor er).

368. Tengo equipaje en la estación.
I have baggage at the station.
ay jaav BAAG-îdch aat thû STEI-shûn.

369. ¿ Quiere usted mandar por mis maletas ?
Will you send for my bags?
huîl yu send for may baagŝ?

370. Aquí tiene usted el talón de mi baúl.
Here is the check for my trunk.
jir îŝ thû chec for may trûnc.

371. Haga el favor de mandar —— a mi cuarto.
Please send —— to my room.
pliŝ send —— tu may rum.

372. Hielo, agua helada.
Ice, ice water.
ais, ais HUOT-ûr.

373. Haga el favor de llamarme a ——.
Please call me at —— o'clock.
pliŝ col mi aat —— ou-CLAC.

374. Quiero el desayuno en mi cuarto.
I want breakfast in my room.
ay huant BREC-fûst în may rum.

375. Haga el favor de conseguirme ——.
Please get me ——.
pliŝ guet mi ——.

376. ¿ Me pueden lavar la ropa ?
Could I have some laundry done?
cûd ay jaav sûm LON-dri dûn?

377. Quiero hacer planchar unos vestidos.
I want some things pressed.
ay huant súm zíngś prest.

378. Mi llave, por favor.
My room key, please.
may rum qui, pliś.

379. ¿ Hay cartas o mensajes para mí ?
Have I any letters or messages?
jaav ay EN-y LET-ûrś or MES-id-chiś?

380. ¿ A qué hora llega el correo ?
When does the mail come in?
huen dûś thú meil cûm ín?

381. ¿ Cuál es el número de mi cuarto?
What is my room number?
huat íś may rum NÚM-bûr?

382. Salgo a ——.
I am leaving at —— o'clock.
ay aam LIV-ing aat —— ou-CLAC.

383. Favor de preparar mi cuenta.
Please make out my bill.
pliś meic aut may bíl.

384. ¿ Se puede guardar aquí el equipaje hasta —— ?
May I store my baggage here until ——?
mey ay stor may BAAG-idch jir ún-TÍL ——?

385. Por favor, reexpídame las cartas a ——.
Please forward my mail to ——.
pliś FOR-u-hûrd may meil tu ——.

CAMARERA
CHAMBERMAID

388. Favor de abrir (cerrar) la ventana.
Please open (close) the window.
pliŝ OU-pen (clouŝ) thû HUÍN-dou.

389. No me moleste hasta ——.
Do not disturb me until ——.
du nat dîs-TÛRB mi ûn-TÍL ——.

390. Favor de cambiar hoy las sábanas.
Please change the sheets today.
pliŝ cheindch thû shits tu-DEY.

391. Tráigame otra (frazada, almohada).
Bring me another (blanket, pillow).
brîng mi û-NÛTH-ûr (BLAAN-quît, PÍL-ou).

392. Una funda, un tapete de baño.
A pillow case, a bath mat.
û PÍL-ou queis, û baaz maat.

393. Ganchos, un vaso, la puerta.
Hangers, a glass, the door.
JAANG-ûrŝ, û glaas, thû dour.

394. Jabón, toallas.   Soap, towels.
soup, TAU-ûlŝ.

395. La bañera o tina, el lavabo.
The bathtub, the washbowl.
thû BAAZ-tûb, thû HUASH-boul.

396. Agua para beber, papel higiénico.
Drinking water, toilet paper.
DRÍN-quîng HUOT-ûr, TOI-let PEI-pûr.

397. ¿ Siempre hay agua caliente ?
Is there always hot water?
îŝ ther OL-huîŝ jat HUOT-ûr?

APARTAMENTO
APARTMENT

401. Quiero un apartamento amueblado.
I want a furnished apartment.
ay huant û FÛR-nîsht û-PART-ment.

402. Sala, dos alcobas.
Living room, two bedrooms.
LÎV-îng rum, tu BED-rumŝ.

403. Un comedor, una cocina.
A dining room, a kitchen.
û DAIN-îng rum, û QUÎ-chen.

404. Un cuarto de baño.
A bathroom.
û BAAZ-rum.

405. ¿ Eso incluye sábanas y mantelería ?
Is the linen furnished?
îŝ thû LÎN-în FÛR-nîsht?

406. ¿ Cuánto es por mes ?
How much is it a month?
jau mûch îŝ ît û mûnz?

407. Las frazadas, los cubiertos de plata,
la vajilla.
The blankets, the silver, dishes.
thû BLAAN-quîts, thû SÎL-vûr, DÎSH-îŝ.

408. **¿ Puedo conseguir una criada ?**
Can I get a maid?
caan ay guet û meid?

409. **¿ Conoce usted a una buena cocinera ?**
Do you know a good cook?
du yu nou û gûd cúc?

410. **¿ Dónde puedo alquilar un garaje ?**
Where can I rent a garage?
huer caan ay rent û gû-RADCH?

RESTAURANTE Y ALIMENTOS
RESTAURANT AND FOOD

413. **¿ Dónde hay un buen restaurante ?**
Where is there a good restaurant?
huer îś ther û gûd RES-tú-rant?

414. **El desayuno, el almuerzo, la comida.**
Breakfast, lunch, dinner.
BREC-fûst, lûnch, DÎN-ûr.

415. **La cena, un sandwich.**
Supper, a sandwich.
SÛP-ûr, û SAAND-huích.

416. **¿ Entre qué horas se sirve la comida ?**
Between what hours is dinner served?
bi-TUIN huat AU-ûrś îś DÎN-ûr sûrvd?

417. **¡Mozo!**   Waiter!   *HUEIT-ûr!*

418. **¿ Podemos almorzar (comer) ahora ?**
Can we have lunch (dinner) now?
caan huy jaav lûnch (DÎN-ûr) nau?

419. La camarera, el camarero, el maitre.
The waitress, the waiter, the headwaiter.
thû HUEIT-res, thû HUEIT-ûr, thû jed HUEIT-ûr.

420. Déme una mesa cerca de la ventana.
Give me a table near the window.
guív mi û TEI-bûl nir thû HUÎN-dou.

421. Al lado, en el rincón.
At the side, in the corner.
aat thû said, ín thû COR-nûr.

422. ¿ Está reservada esta mesa ?
Is this table reserved?
íß thís TEI-bûl ri-ŝÛRVD ?

423. Aquélla estará desocupada dentro de poco.
That one will be free soon.
thaat huon huîl bi fri sun.

424. Deseamos comer a la carta.
We want to dine à la carte.
huy huant tu dain a la cart.

425. Haga el favor de servirnos de prisa.
Please serve us quickly.
pliŝ ʼsûrv ûs CUÎC-li.

426. Tráigame el menú (la carta de vinos).
Bring me the menu (the wine list).
bríng mi thû MEN-yu (thû huain líst).

427. Una servilleta, un vaso.
A napkin, a glass.
û NAAP-quín, û glaas.

428. Un plato, un cuchillo.
  A plate, a knife.
  û pleit, û naif.

429. Un tenedor, una cuchara.
  A fork, a large spoon.
  û forc, û lardch spun.

430. Una cucharita, el pan.
  A teaspoon, the bread.
  û TI-spun, thû bred.

431. La mantequilla, la crema.
  The butter, the cream.
  thû BÛT-ûr, thû crim.

432. El azúcar, la sal, la pimienta.
  The sugar, the salt, the pepper.
  thû SHÛG-ûr, thû solt, thû PEP-pûr.

433. La salsa, el aceite, el vinagre.
  The sauce, the oil, the vinegar.
  thû sos, thi oil, thû VÎN-î-gûr.

434. Esto no está limpio.   This is not clean.
  thîs îs nat clin.

435. Está sucio.   It is dirty.   *ît îs DÛR-ti.*

436. Un poco más de esto.
  A little more of this.
  û LÎT-ûl mor ûv thîs

437. Basta, gracias.
  I have had enough, thanks.
  ay jaav jaad i-NÛF, zaancs.

438. Me gusta la carne (poco cocida, bien cocida).
I like the meat (rare, well done).
ay laic thû mit (rer, huel dûn).

439. Esto está demasiado cocido (no está bastante cocido).
This is overcooked (undercooked).
this îs ou-vûr-CÚCT (ûn-dûr-CÚCT).

440. Esto está muy (duro, dulce, agrio).
This is too (tough, sweet, sour).
this îs tu (túf, suit, SAU-ûr).

441. Esto está frío.   This is cold.
this îs could.

442. Lléveselo.   Take it away.
teic ît û-HUEY.

443. No he pedido esto.
I did not order this.
ay dîd nat OR-dûr this.

444. ¿ Se puede cambiar esto por —— ?
May I change this for —— ?
may ay cheindch this for —— ?

445. Pida al maitre que venga acá.
Ask the head waiter to come here.
aasc thû jed HUEIT-ûr tu cûm jir.

446. La cuenta, por favor.
The check, please.
thû chec, pliŝ.

447. Haga el favor de pagar en la caja.
Kindly pay at the cashier's.
CAIND-li pey aat thû caash-IRŜ.

448. ¿ Está incluída la propina ?
Is the tip included ?
iŝ thû tîp în-CLUD-id?

449. ¿ Hay que pagar por el servicio ?
Is there a service charge ?
iŝ ther û SÛRV-iŝ chardch ?

450. El cambio es para usted.
Keep the change.
quip thû cheindch.

451. Hay un error en la cuenta.
There is a mistake in the bill.
ther iŝ û mîs-TEIC în thû bîl.

452. ¿ Qué cubren estos cargos ?
What are these charges for ?
huat ar thiŝ CHARD-chiŝ for ?

CAFÉ
CAFÉ

455. Cantinero, un coctel.
Bartender, a cocktail.
BAR-ten-dûr, û CAC-teil.

456. Una bebida no alcohólica.
A soft drink.
û soft drînc.

457. Una bebida de fruta.   A fruit drink.
û frut drînc.

458. Una botella (**pequeña, grande**) de "**ginger ale.**"

A (small, large) bottle of ginger ale.

û (smol, laardch) BAT-ûl ûv DCHÎN-dchûr heil.

459. Un vaso de ——. A glass of ——.

û glaas ûv ——.

460. Cerveza (**clara, oscura**).

(Light, dark) beer.

(lait, daarc) bir.

461. Whisky (**con soda**).

Whiskey (and soda).

HUÎS-qui (aand SOU-dû).

462. Vino tinto, vino blanco.

Red wine, white wine.

red huain, huait huain.

463. Aguardiente. Brandy. *BRAAN-di.*

464. Tomemos otro más.

Let's have another.

lets jaav û-NÛTH-ûr.

ALIMENTOS
FOOD

467. Caldo (**de pollo, con legumbres**).

(Chicken, vegetable) soup.

(CHÎ-quín, VEDCH-tû-búl) sup.

468. Huevos (**revueltos, fritos**).

(Scrambled, fried) eggs.

(SCRAAM-búld, fraid) egŝ.

469. Huevos (escalfados, duros).
(Soft-boiled, hard-boiled) eggs.
(*soft-boild, jard-boild) egŝ.*

470. Tortilla de huevos.   Omelet.   *AM-let.*

ENTRADA: CARNES Y PESCADO
ENTREE: MEATS AND FISH

471. Carne asada.   Roast beef.   *roust bif.*

472. Carpa.   Carp.   *carp.*

473. Pollo (asado, frito)
Chicken (roast, fried).
CHÎ-quín (roust, fraid).

474. Pato.   Duck.   *dúc.*

475. Ganso.   Goose.   *gus.*

476. Carne de carnero.   Lamb.   *laam.*

477. Hígado.   Liver.   *LÎV-ûr.*

478. Langosta.   Lobster.   *LAB-stûr.*

479. Carne de puerco.   Pork.   *porc.*

480. Camarones.   Shrimp.   *shrímp.*

481. Biftec.   Steak.   *steic.*

482. Rebanada de ——.   Slice of -——.
slais ûv ——.

483. Sardina.   Sardine.   *sar-DIN.*

484. Salmón.   Salmon.   *SAA-mún.*

485. Longaniza o chorizo o salchicha.
Sausage.
SOS-îdch.

486. Carne de ternera. Veal. *vil.*

LEGUMBRES, ENSALADA Y FRUTAS
VEGETABLES, SALAD AND FRUIT

487. Espárragos. Asparagus.
aas-PAAR-û-gûs.

488. Frijoles o habichuelas. Beans.
binŝ.

489. Col. Cabbage. *CAAB-îdch.*

490. Berza ácida. Sauerkraut.
SAU-ûr-craut.

491. Coliflor. Cauliflower. *COL-i-flau-ûr.*

492. Zanahorias. Carrots. *CAAR-ûts.*

493. Maíz. Corn. *corn.*

494. Pepino. Cucumber. *QUIU-cûm-búr.*

495. Ajo. Garlic. *GAR-lîc.*

496. Lechuga. Lettuce. *LET-îs.*

497. Setas. Mushrooms. *MÛSH-rumŝ.*

498. Cebolla. Onion. *ÛN-yûn.*

499. Guisantes. Peas. *piŝ.*

500. Pimientos. Peppers. *PEP-pûrŝ.*

501. Patatas fritas. Fried potatoes.
fraid po-TEI-touŝ.

502. Patatas cocidas. Boiled potatoes.
boild po-TEI-touŝ.

503. Puré de papas. Mashed potatoes.
maasht po-TEI-touŝ.

504. Rábanos. Radishes. *RAAD-îsh-eŝ.*

505. Espinacas. Spinach. *SPÎN-îch.*

506. Tomates. Tomatoes. *to-MEI-touŝ.*

507. Manzana. Apple. *AAP-ûl.*

508. Compota de manzana. Applesauce.
AAP-ûl-sos.

509. Uvas. Grapes. *greips.*

510. Toronja. Grapefruit. *GREIP-frut.*

511. Limón. Lemon. *LEM-ûn.*

512. Melón. Melon. *MEL-ûn*

513. Sandía. Watermelon.
HUOT-ûr-mel-ûn.

514. Nueces. Nuts. *nûts.*

515. Cacahuates. Peanuts. *PI-nûts.*

516. Nueces. Walnuts. *HUOL-nûts.*

517. Aceitunas (negras, verdes).
(Ripe, green) olives.
(raip, grin) AL-îvŝ.

518. Naranja. Orange. *AR-endch.*

519. Melocotón. Peach. *pich.*

520. Pasas. Raisins. *REIŜ-înŝ.*

521. Frambuesas. Raspberries.
RAAŜ-ber-iŝ.

522. Fresas. Strawberries. *STRO-ber-iŝ.*

523. Cerezas. Cherries. *CHER-iŝ.*

BEBIDAS
BEVERAGES

524. Café. Coffee. *COF-y.*

525. Limonada. Lemonade. *lem-ûn-EID.*

526. Leche. Milk. *mîlc.*

527. Té (con limón, con crema).
Tea (with lemon, with cream).
ti (huîth LEM-ûn, huîth crim).

528. Gaseosa. Soda pop. *SOU-dû pap.*

POSTRES
DESSERTS

529. Torta. Cake. *quec.*

530. Bizcochitos. Cookies. *CU-quiŝ.*

531. Chocolate. Chocolate. *CHOC-lît.*

532. Vainilla. Vanilla. *vû-NÎL-û.*

533. Flan. Custard. *CÛS-tûrd.*

534. Helado. Ice cream. *ais crim.*

535. Conserva. Jam. *dchaam.*

536. Jalea. Jelly. *DCHEL-y.*

MISCELÁNEO
MISCELLANEOUS

537. Queso. Cheese. *chiŝ.*

538. Mostaza. Mustard. *MÛS-tûrd.*

539. Fideos. Noodles. *NU-dûlŝ.*

540. Arroz. Rice. *rais.*

541. Avena. Oatmeal. *OUT-mil.*

542. Tostada. Toast. *toust.*

IGLESIA
PLACES OF WORSHIP

544. Iglesia (católica, anglicana).
(Catholic, Anglican) church.
(CAAẐ-o-lîc, AAN-glî-cún) chúrch.

545. Una iglesia protestante.
A Protestant church.
û PRAT-es-tûnt chúrch.

546. Una sinagoga. A synagogue.
û SÎN-û-gog.

547. ¿ Dónde predican en (alemán, italiano, español) ?
Where is there a service in (German, Italian, Spanish)?
huer îŝ ther û SÛR-vîs in (DCHÛR-mûn, i-TAAL-yûn, SPAAN-îsh) ?

548. ¿A qué hora es (el servicio, la misa)?
When is the (service, mass)?
huen îŝ thû (SÛR-vîs, maas)?

549. ¿Hay algún cura que hable (alemán, italiano, español)?
Is there a (German, Italian, Spanish)-speaking priest?
îŝ ther û (DCHÛR-mún, î-TAAL-yûn, SPAAN-îsh)-SPI-quîng prist?

550. Un rabino.   Un clérigo.
Rabbi.   Minister.
RAAB-ay.   MÎN-îs-tûr.

FIESTAS
HOLIDAYS

551. Navidad.   Año Nuevo.   Pascuas.
Christmas.   New Year's.   Easter.
CRÎS-mûs.   niu yirŝ.   IST-ûr.

VISITAS A PUNTOS DE INTERÉS
SIGHTSEEING

553. Deseo un guía que hable ——.
I want a guide who speaks ——.
ay huant û gaid ju spics ——.

554. ¿Cuánto cobra usted (por hora, al día)?
What is the charge (per hour, per day)?
huat îŝ thû chardch (pûr AU-ûr, pûr dey)?

555. Artesanía indígena.
Native arts and crafts.
NEI-tîv arts aand craafts.

556. La pintura, la escultura.
Painting, sculpture.
PEINT-ing, SCULP-chûr.

557. ¿Tendré yo tiempo para visitar los museos?
Shall I have time to visit the museums?
shaal ay jaav taim tu VÎS-ît thû miu-SÎ-ûmŝ?

558. La catedral, el ayuntamiento.
The cathedral, the city hall.
thû caa-ZI-drûl, thû SÎ-ti jol.

559. El río, el lago.
The river, the lake.
thû RÎV-ûr, thû leic.

560. ¿Está abierta (todavía)?
Is it (still) open?
îŝ ît (stîl) OU-pen?

561. ¿Hasta qué hora está abierto?
How long does it stay open?
jau long dûŝ ît stey OU-pen?

562. ¿Cuánto tiempo tengo que esperar?
How long must I wait?
jau long mûst ay hueit?

563. ¿Dónde está la (entrada, salida)?
Where is the (entrance, exit)?
huer îŝ thi (EN-trûns, ECS-ît)?

564. ¿ Cuánto se paga por entrar ?
What is the price of admission?
huat íŝ thû prais ûv aad-MÍSH-ûn?

565. ¿ Necesitamos un guía ?
Do we need a guide?
du huy nid û gaid?

566. ¿ Cuánto cuesta la guía ?
How much is the guidebook?
jau mûch íŝ thû GAID-búc?

567. ¿ Se permite sacar fotografías ?
May I take photographs?
mey ay teic FOU-tû-graafs?

568. ¿ Vende postales ?
Do you sell post cards?
du yu sel poust cards?

569. ¿ Tiene un libro sobre —— ?
Do you have a book about —— ?
du yu jaav û búc û-BAUT —— ?

570. Lléveme al hotel.
Take me back to the hotel.
teic mi baac tu thû jou-TEL.

571. Regrese por ——.
Go back by way of ——.
gou baac bay huey̌ ûv ——.

DIVERSIONES
AMUSEMENTS

574. Un concierto, el cine.
A concert, movies.
û CAN-sûrt, MU-viŝ.

575. La playa, el tenis, las carreras de caballos.
The beach, tennis, horseracing.
thû bich, TEN-îs, JORS-reis-îng.

576. Esquiar, patinar. Skiing, skating.
SQUI-îng, SQUEIT-îng.

577. Un cabaret, la ópera, el teatro.
A night club, the opera, the theater.
û nait clûb, thi AP-ûr-û, thû ZI-û-tûr.

578. ¿Hay función esta tarde?
Is there a matinée today?
îŝ ther û maa-tî-NEY tû-DEY?

579. ¿A qué hora comienza la (función, variedad)?
When does the (performance, floor-show) start?
huen dûŝ thû (pûr-FORM-ûns, FLOR-shou) start?

580. El cubierto, el mínimo.
Cover charge, minimum.
CÛV-ûr chardch, MÎN-î-mûm.

581. ¿Adónde podemos ir a bailar?
Where can we go to dance?
huer caan huy gou tu daans?

582. ¿Hay localidades para esta noche?
Have you any seats for tonight?
jaav yu EN-y sits for tû-NAIT?

583. Una butaca, un asiento reservado.
An orchestra seat, a reserved seat.
aan OR-ques-trû sit, û ri-SÛRVD sit.

584. En el anfiteatro, el palco.
In the balcony, the box.
în thû BAAL-cû-ni, thû bacs.

585. ¿Puedo ver (oír) bien desde allí?
Can I see (hear) well from there?
caan ay si (jir) huel frûm ther?

586. No muy (cerca, lejos).
Not too (near, far).
nat tu (nir, far).

587. La música es excelente.
The music is excellent.
thû MIU-sîc îs EC-sû-lûnt.

588. Eso es muy (interesante, cómico).
That is very (interesting, funny).
thaat îs VER-y (ÎN-tûr-est·îng, FÛN-y).

589. ¿Me permite esta pieza?
May I have this dance?
mey ay jaav thîs daans?

590. ¿Es ahora intermedio?
Is this the intermission?
îs thîs thî în-tûr-MÎSH-ûn?

COMPRAS Y SERVICIOS
SHOPPING AND PERSONAL
  SERVICES

593. Deseo ir de compras.
I want to go shopping.
ay huant tu gou SHAP-ing.

594. ¿Dónde está la panadería?
Where is the bakery?
huer iŝ thû BEI-cûr-y?

595. Una dulcería, una tabaquería.
A candy store, a cigar store.
û CAAN-di stor, û si-GAR stor.

596. Un almacén de ropa, un almacén.
A clothing store, a department store.
û CLOUTH-ing stor, û di-PART-ment stor.

597. Una farmacia, una tienda de comestibles.
A drug store, a grocery.
û drûg stor, û GROU-sûr-y.

598. Una ferretería, una sombrería.
A hardware store, a hat shop.
û JARD-huer stor, û jaat shap.

599. Una joyería, una zapatería.
A jewelry store, a shoe store.
û DCHU-el-ri stor, û shu stor.

600. Una carnicería, una sastrería.
A meat market, a tailor shop.
û mit MAR-quît, û TEI-lor shap.

601. Zapatero, relojero.
Shoemaker, watchmaker.
SHU-meic-ûr, HUACH-meic-ûr.

602. Venta, ganga.   Sale, bargain sale.
seil, BAR-guen seil.

603. Quiero comprar ——.
I want to buy ——.
ay huant tu bay ——.

604. (No) me gusta esto.
I (do not) like this.
ay (du nat) laic thîs.

605. ¿Cuánto cuesta eso?
How much is that?
jáu mûch îs thaat?

606. Es (muy) caro.
It is (very) expensive.
ît îs (VER-y) ecs-PEN-sîv.

607. Prefiero algo mejor (más barato).
I prefer something better (cheaper).
ay pri-FÛR SÛM-zîng BET-ûr (CHIP-ûr).

608. Muéstreme otros.
Show me some others.
shou mi sûm ÛTH-ûrs.

609. ¿Me permite probarme esto?
May I try this on?
mey ay tray thîs an?

610. ¿Puedo mandar hacer uno?
Can I order one?
caan ay OR-dûr huon?

611. ¿Cuánto tardará?
How long will it take?
jau long huíl ît teic?

**612. Haga el favor de tomarme las medi-
das.**
Please take my measurements.
plîŝ teic may MEŜH-ûr-ments.

614. No me queda bien. It does not fit.
ît dûŝ nat fît.

615. Es demasiado (largo, corto).
It is too (long, short).
ît îŝ tu (long, short).

616. (No) me va bien.
It is (not) becoming to me.
ît îŝ (nat) bi-CÚM-îng tu mi.

617. Hágame el favor de envolver esto.
Will you wrap this, please.
huíl yu raap thîs, plîŝ.

618. ¿A quién pago?
Whom do I pay?
jum du ay pey?

619. ¿Puede usted mandar esto a —— ?
Can you ship this to —— ?
caan yu shîp thîs tu —— ?

620. Haga el favor de enviarme una cuenta.
Please bill me.
plîŝ bîl mi.

CASA DE CORREOS
POST OFFICE

621. ¿Dónde está la casa de correos?
Where is the post office?
huer îs thû poust OF-îs?

622. ¿Una tarjeta postal (carta) para —— ?
A post card (letter) to —— ?
û poust card (LET-ûr) tu —— ?

623. ¿Cuántas estampillas necesito?
How many stamps do I need?
jau MEN-y staamps du ay nid?

624. Cuatro estampillas de tres centavos.
Four three-cent stamps.
for ZRI-sent staamps.

**625. No hay nada sujeto a impuesto en
esto.**
There is nothing dutiable in this.
ther îs NÛZ-îng DIU-tî-û-bûl în this.

626. ¿Saldrá esto hoy?
Will this go out today?
huîl this gou aut tû-DEY?

627. Déme un recibo, por favor.
Give me a receipt, please.
guîv mi û ri-SIT, plîs.

628. Quiero mandar un giro postal.
I want to send a money order.
ay huant tu send û MÛN-y OR-dûr.

629. ¿A qué ventanilla voy?
To which window dò I go?
tu huích HUÍN-dou du ay gou?

630. Por correo aéreo, paquete postal.
By airmail, parcel post.
bay er meil, PAR-sûl poust.

631. Certificado, entrega inmediata.
Registered, special delivery.
RED-chîs-tûrd, SPESH-ûl dû-LÍV-ûr-y.

632. Asegurado.   Insured.   *în-SHURD.*

BANCO
BANK

634. ¿Dónde está el banco más cercano?
Where is the nearest bank?
huer îs thû NIR-est baanc?

635. ¿En qué ventanilla puedo cobrar esto?
At which window can I cash this?
aat huích HUÍN-dou caan ay caash thîs?

636. ¿Puede usted cambiarme esto?
Can you change this for me?
caan yu cheindch thîs for mi?

637. ¿Quiere usted cobrarme un cheque?
Will you cash a check?
huíl yu caash û chec?

638. Favor de no darme billetes grandes.
Do not give me large bills.
du nat guîv me lardch bîlŝ.

639. ¿Puede usted darme cambio?
May I have some change?
mey ay jaav sûm cheindch?

640. Carta de crédito.   Letter of credit.
LET-ûr úv CRED-ît.

641. Tengo cheques para viajeros.
I have travelers' checks.
ay jaav TRAAV-lûrŝ checs.

642. Un giro.   A bank draft.   *û baanc draaft.*

LIBRERÍA Y PAPELERÍA
BOOKSTORE AND STATIONER'S

646. ¿Dónde hay una librería?
Where is there a bookstore?
huer îŝ ther û BÛC-stor?

**647. Una papelería, un puesto de perió-
dicos.**
A stationer's, a news stand.
û STEI-shûn-ûrŝ, û niuŝ staand.

648. Periódicos, revistas, semanarios.
Newspapers, magazines, weeklies.
NIUŜ-pei-pûrŝ, maag-û-ŜINŜ, HUIC-liŝ.

649. Tarjetas postales, naipes.
Post cards, playing cards.
poust cardŝ, PLEI-îng cardŝ.

650. Tarjetas de felicitación.
Greeting cards.
GRIT-îng cardŝ.

651. Papel para cartas, tinta, papel secante.
Writing paper, ink, blotter.
RAIT-ing PEI-púr, ínc, BLAT-úr.

652. Sobres para correo aéreo, un lápiz.
Air mail envelopes, a pencil.
er meil EN-vú-loups, û PEN-síl.

653. Un diccionario, una guía.
A dictionary, a guide book.
û DÍC-shún-er-y, û gaid búc.

654. Un mapa de ——.   A map of ——.
û maap úv ——.

655. Una pluma fuente, artículos para pintores.
A fountain pen, artist's materials.
û FAUN-tín pen, AR-tîsts mû-TÍ-riûlŝ.

656. Cuerda (fuerte), una goma para borrar.
(Strong) string, an eraser.
(strong) stríng, aan i-REIS-úr.

657. Cinta para máquina, papel carbón.
Typewriter ribbon, carbon paper.
TAIP-rait-úr RÍB-ún, CAR-bún PEI-púr.

658. Papel de seda, papel para envolver.
Tissue paper, wrapping paper.
TÍSH-u PEI-púr, RAAP-íng PEI-púr.

TABAQUERÍA
CIGAR STORE

661. ¿ Dónde está la tabaquería más cercana ?
Where is the nearest cigar store?
huer îŝ thû NIR-est sî-GAR stor?

662. Quisiera unos cigarros.
I want some cigars.
ay huant sûm sî-GARŜ.

663. Un paquete de cigarrillos, por favor.
A pack of cigarettes, please.
û paac ûv sîg-û-RETS, pliŝ.

664. Por favor, muéstreme algunas petacas.
Please show me some cigarette cases.
pliŝ shou mi sûm sîg-û-RET QUEIS-îŝ.

665. Necesito un encendedor.
I need a lighter.
ay nid û LAIT-ûr.

666. Piedra (de encendedor), líquido.
Flint, fluid.
flînt, FLU-îd.

667. Fósforos, una pipa.
Matches, a pipe.
MAACH-îŝ, û paip.

668. Tabaco, una bolsa para tabaco.
Pipe tobacco, a pouch.
paip to-BAAC-ou, û pauch.

PELUQUERÍA Y SALÓN DE BELLEZA
BARBER SHOP AND BEAUTY PARLOR

671. **¿Dónde hay un buen peluquero?**
Where is there a good barber?
huer îŝ ther û gûd BAR-bŭr?

672. **Quisiera que me (cortara el pelo, afeitara).**
I want a (hair cut, shave).
ay huant û (JER-cût, sheiv).

673. **No muy corto.**
Not too short.
nat tu short.

674. **No corte de arriba.**
Do not cut any off the top.
du nat cût EN-y of thû tap.

675. **(No) ponga pomada.**
(Do not) put on oil.
(du nat) pût an oil.

676. **Me hago la raya al lado (al otro lado).**
I part my hair on the side (on the other side).
ay part may jer an thû said (an thi ÛTH-ŭr said).

677. **En medio.** In the middle.
în thû MÎD-ûl.

678. **El agua está muy (caliente, fría).**
The water is too (hot, cold).
thû HUOT-ŭr îŝ tu (jat, could).

679. Quiero hacerme lustrar los zapatos.
I want my shoes shined.
ay huant may shuŝ shaind.

680. ¿ Puedo hacer una cita para ——— ?
Can I make an appointment for ——— ?
caan ay meic aan aa-POINT-ment for ——— ?

681. Quiero un champú.
I want a shampoo.
ay huant û shaam-PU.

682. Un peinado al agua, un permanente.
A finger wave, a permanent.
û FÎNG-ûr hueiv, û PÛR-mû-nent.

683. Un masaje, una manicura.
A facial, a manicure.
û FEI-shûl, û MAAN-î-quiur.

FOTOGRAFÍA
PHOTOGRAPHY

686. Quiero un rollo de película (de color).
I want a roll of (color) film.
ay huant û roul ûv (CÛL-ûr) film.

687. El tamaño es ———.   The size is ———.
thû saiŝ îŝ ———.

688. Un rollo de película de cine, para esta cámara.
Movie film, for this camera.
MUV-y film, for thîs CAAM-ûr-û.

689. ¿Cuánto cuesta revelar un rollo?
What is the charge for developing a roll?
huat îs thû chardch for di-VEL-ûp-îng û roul?

690. Por una copia de cada negativo.
For one print of each.
for huon prínt ûv ich.

691. Por una amplificación.
For an enlargement.
for aan en-LARDCH-ment.

692. La cámara está decompuesta.
The camera is out of order.
thû CAAM-ûr-û îs aut ûv OR-dûr.

693. ¿Cuándo estarán listas?
When will they be ready?
huen huîl they bi RED-y?

694. ¿Se alquilan cámaras?
Do you rent cameras?
du yu rent CAAM-ûr-ûs?

695. Quisiera una para hoy.
I should like one for today.
ay shûd laic huon for tû-DEY.

LAVANDERÍA Y TINTORERÍA
LAUNDRY AND DRY CLEANING

698. ¿Dónde está (la lavandería, la tintorería) más cercana?
Where is the nearest (laundry, dry cleaner)?
huer îs thû NIR-est (LON-dri, drai CLIN-ûr)?

699. Para hacer (lavar, remendar).
To be (washed, mended).
tu bi (huasht, MEN-díd).

700. Para hacer (limpiar, planchar).
To be (cleaned, pressed).
tu bi (clind, prest).

701. No lave esto en agua caliente.
Do not wash this in hot water.
du nat huash thís ín jat HUOT-ûr.

702. Use agua tibia.
Use lukewarm water.
yuś LUC-huorm HUOT-ûr.

703. Tenga mucho-cuidado.
Be very careful.
bi VER-y QUER-fúl.

704. No almidone los cuellos.
Do not starch the collars.
du nat starch thû CAL-ûrŝ.

705. ¿Cuándo puedo tener esto?
When can I have this?
huen caan ay jaav thís?

706. Aquí tiene usted la lista.
Here is the list.
jir íŝ thû lîst.

707. Falta el cinturón.
The belt is missing.
thû belt íŝ MÍS-íng.

VESTIDOS
CLOTHING

711. Delantal. Apron. *HEI-prûn.*

712. Gorra de baño. Bathing cap.
BEITH-îng caap.

713. Traje de baño. Bathing suit.
BEITH-îng sut.

714. Blusa. Blouse. *blaus.*

715. Sostén. Brassiere. *brû-ŜIR.*

716. Abrigo o saco. Coat. *cout.*

717. Cuello. Collar. *CAL-ûr.*

718. Pañales. Diapers. *DAI-pûrŝ.*

719. Vestido. Dress. *dres.*

720. Ligas. Garters. *GAR-tûrŝ.*

721. Guantes. Gloves. *glûvŝ.*

722. Pañuelo. Handkerchief.
ĴAAN-cûr-chíf.

723. Sombrero. Hat. *jaat.*

724. Chaqueta. Jacket. *DCHAA-quet.*

725. Corbata. Necktie. *NEC-tay.*

726. Camisón. Nightgown. *NAIT-gaun.*

727. Gabán. Overcoat. *OU-vûr-cout.*

728. Pijama. Pajamas. *pûd-CHA-mûŝ.*

729. Calzones. Panties. *PAAN-tiŝ.*

730. Enaguas. Petticoat. *PET-i-cout.*

731. Impermeable. Raincoat. *REIN-cout.*

732. Traje de montar. Riding clothes.
RAID-íng clouŝ.

733. Bata. Robe. *roub.*

734. Camisa. Shirt. *shûrt.*

735. Calzoncillos. Shorts. *shorts.*

736. Camiseta. Undershirt. *ÛN-dûr-shûrt.*

737. Refajo. Slip. *slîp.*

738. Pantuflas. Slippers. *SLÎP-ûrŝ.*

739. Calcetines. Socks. *sacs.*

740. Medias de nylon. Nylon stockings.
NAI-lan STA-quíngŝ.

741. Traje. Suit. *sut.*

742. Tirantes. Suspenders. *sûs-PEND-ûrŝ.*

743. Suéter. Sweater. *SUET-ûr.*

744. Pantalones. Trousers. *TRAU-ŝûrŝ.*

745. Ropa interior. Underwear.
ÛN-dûr-huer.

746. Chaleco. Vest. *vest.*

SALUD Y ACCIDENTES
HEALTH AND ACCIDENTS

749. Hubo un accidente.
There has been an accident.
ther jaaŝ bîn aan AAC-ŝi-dent.

750. Llame a (un médico, una enfermera.)
Get (a doctor, a nurse).
guet {û DAC-tûr, û nûrs).

751. Mande buscar una ambulancia.
Send for an ambulance.
send for aan AAM-biu-lûns.

752. Por favor, traiga unas frazadas.
Please bring blankets.
pliŝ brîng BLAAN-quîts.

753. Una camilla, agua.
A stretcher, water.
û STRETCH-ûr, HUOT-ûr.

754. Está (gravemente) herido.
He is (seriously) injured.
ji îŝ (SI-ri-ûs-li) ÎND-chûrd.

755. Ayúdeme a cargarlo.
Help me carry him.
jelp mi CAAR-y jîm.

756. Fué atropellado.
He was knocked down.
ji huaŝ nact daun.

757. Ella se cayó (se desmayó).
She has fallen (fainted).
shi jaaŝ FOL-en (FEIN-ted).

758. Me estoy desmayando.
I feel faint.
ay fil feint.

759. Tiene (una fractura, contusión, herida).
He has (a fracture, bruise, cut).
ji jaas (û FRAAC-chúr, brus, cût).

760. Él (se quemó, se cortó) la mano.
He has (burned, cut) his hand.
ji jaas (bûrnt, cût) jîs jaand.

761. Está (sangrando, hinchado).
It is (bleeding, swollen).
ît îs (BLID-îng, SUO-len).

762. ¿Puede hacerme una curación?
Can you dress this?
caan yu dres thîs?

763. ¿Tiene usted (vendajes, tablillas)?
Have you any (bandages, splints)?
jaav yu EN-y (BAAN-dîd-chîs, splînts)?

764. Necesito algo para un torniquete.
I need something for a tourniquet.
ay nid SÛM-zîng for û TÛR-nî-quet.

765. ¿Está usted bien?
Are you all right?
ar yu ol rait?

766. Me duele aquí.
It hurts here.
ît jûrts jir.

767. Quiero sentarme un momento.
I want to sit down a moment.
ay huant tu sît daun û MOU-ment.

768. No puedo mover el ——.
I cannot move my ——.
ay caan-NAT muv may ——.

769. Me lastimé el ——.
I have hurt my ——.
ay jaav jûrt may ——.

770. ¿Puedo viajar el lunes?
Can I travel on Monday?
caan ay TRAAV-úl an MÛN-dey?

771. Sírvase avisar a mi (marido, esposa).
Please notify my (husband, wife).
pliŝ NOU-tî-fay may (JÛŜ-bînd, huaif).

772. Aquí tiene usted mi (cédula de identidad, tarjeta).
Here is my (identification, card).
jir îŝ may (ai-den-tî-fî-QUEI-shûn, card).

ENFERMEDAD
ILLNESS

775. Deseo ver a un (doctor, especialista).
I wish to see a (doctor, specialist).
ay huîsh tu si û (DAC-tûr, SPESH-úl-îst).

776. Un médico (alemán, italiano, español).
A (German, Italian, Spanish) doctor.
û (DCHÛR-mûn, î-TAAL-yûn, SPAAN-îsh) DAC-tûr.

777. No duermo bien.
I do not sleep well.
ay du nat slip huel.

778. Me duele el pie. My foot hurts.
may fût jûrts.

779. Tengo dolor de cabeza.
My head aches.
may jed heics.

780. Tengo un absceso.
I have an abscess.
ay jaav aan AAB-ses.

781. Apendicitis, ataque de bilis.
Appendicitis, biliousness.
aa-pen-dî-SAI-tîs, BÎL-yûs-nes.

782. Picadura, ampolla.
Insect bite, blister.
ÎN-sect bait, BLÎS-tûr.

783. Un divieso, una quemadura.
A boil, a burn.
û boil, û bûrn.

784. Escalofríos, un catarro.
Chills, a cold.
chîlŝ, û could.

785. Estreñimiento, una tos.
Constipation, a cough.
can-stî-PEI-shûn, û cof.

786. Un calambre, diarrea.
A cramp, diarrhea.
û craamp, dai-û-RI-û.

787. Disentería, un dolor de oído.
Dysentery, an earache.
DÎS-en-ter-y, aan IR-eic.

788. Una calentura, envenenamiento.
A fever, food poisoning.
û FI-vûr, fud POI-ŝûn-íng.

789. Ronquera, indigestión.
Hoarseness, indigestion.
JORS-nes, ín-DÍD-ches-chûn.

790. Náuseas, pulmonía.
Nausea, pneumonia.
NOSH-û, niu-MOUN-yû.

**791. Inflamación de la garganta, dolorido
o enconado.**
A sore throat, sore.
û sor zrout, sor.

792. Rozado, una torcedura.
Chafed, a sprain.
cheift, û sprein.

793. Quemadura de sol, insolación.
Sunburn, sunstroke.
SÛN-bûrn, SÛN-strouc.

794. Fiebre tifoidea, vomitar.
Typhoid fever, to vomit.
TAI-foid FI-vûr, tu VAM-ît.

795. ¿Qué debo hacer?
What am I to do?
juat aam ay tu du?

796. ¿Tengo que guardar cama?
Must I stay in bed?
mûst ay stey ín bed?

797. ¿Tengo que ir a un hospital?
Do I have to go to a hospital?
du ay jaav tu gou tu û JAS-pî-túl?

798. ¿Puedo levantarme?
May I get up?
mey ay guet úp?

799. Me siento mejor.
I feel better.
ay fil BET-ûr.

800. ¿Cuándo cree usted que me sentiré mejor?
When do you think I'll be better?
huen du yu thínc ail bi BET-ûr?

801. ¿Cuándo vuelve usted?
When will you come again?
huen huîl yu cûm û-GUEN?

802. Una gota, una cucharadita.
A drop, a teaspoonful.
û drap, û TI-spun-fúl.

803. Agua caliente, hielo, medicina.
Hot water, ice, medicine.
jat HUOT-ûr, ais, MED-î-sîn.

804. Una píldora, una receta.
A pill, a prescription.
û pîl, û prî-SCRÍP-shún.

805. Cada hora, (antes, después) de las comidas.
Every hour, (before, after) meals.
EV-ri AU-ûr, (bi-FOR, AAF-tûr) milŝ.

806. Dos veces al día. Twice a day.
tuais û dey.

807. Al acostarse, al levantarse.
On going to bed, on getting up.
an GOU-ing tu bed, an GUET-ing ûp.

808. Una radiografía. X-ray. *ECS-rey.*

DENTISTA
DENTIST

811. ¿Conoce usted a un buen dentista?
Do you know a good dentist?
du yu nou û gûd DEN-tîst?

812. Me duele este diente.
This tooth hurts.
thîs tuz jûrts.

813. ¿Puede usted componerlo (por ahora)?
Can you fix it (temporarily)?
caan yu fîcs ît (tem-pû-RER-î-li)?

814. Perdí una tapadura.
I have lost a filling.
ay jaav lost û FÎL-îng.

815. Me rompí un diente.
I have broken a tooth.
ay jaav BROU-quen û tuz.

816. No quiero que me lo saque.
I do not want it extracted.
ay du nat huant ît ecs-TRAAC-ted.

**817. ¿Puede usted componer esta denta-
dura ?**

Can you repair this denture?
caan yu ri-PER thîs DEN-chûr?

818. Un anestésico local.

A local anesthetic.
û LOU-cûl aan-es-ZET-îc.

FARMACIA
DRUGSTORE

821. ¿Dónde hay una farmacia ?

Where is there a drugstore?
huer îs ther. û DRÛG-stor?

822. ¿Puede prepararme esta receta ?

Can you fill this prescription?
caan yu fîl thîs prî-SCRÎP-shûn?

823. ¿Cuánto tiempo tardará ?

How long will it take?
jau long huîl ît teic?

824. Quiero esparadrapo.

I want adhesive tape.
ay huant aad-JI-sîv teip.

825. Alcohol, un antiséptico, aspirina.

Alcohol, an antiseptic, aspirin.
AAL-co-jol, aan aan-tî-SEP-tîc, AAS-pî-rîn.

826. Analgésico, vendas.

Analgesic, bandages.
aan-aald-CHI-sîc, BAAN-dîd-chîs.

827. Bicarbonato de soda.
Bicarbonate of soda.
bai-CAR-bûn-eit ûv SOU-dû.

828. Ácido bórico, un cepillo (de dientes).
Boric acid, a hair (tooth) brush.
BOU-rîc AAS-îd, û jer (tuz) brûsh.

829. Ácido fénico, aceite de ricino.
Carbolic acid, castor oil.
car-BAL-îc AAS-îd, CAAS-tûr oil.

**830. Líquido para desmanchar, crema cos-
mética.**
Cleaning fluid, cold cream.
CLIN-îng FLU-îd, could crim.

**831. Un peine, parches para los callos,
algodón.**
A comb, corn pads, cotton.
û coum, corn paadŝ, CAT-ûn.

832. Un depilatorio, un deodorante.
A depilatory, a deodorant.
û di-PÎL-û-to-ri, û di-OU-dûr-ûnt.

833. Tapones para el oído, sal inglesa.
Ear stoppers, Epsom salts.
ir STAP-ûrŝ, EP-sûm solts.

**834. Una copilla para los ojos, gasa, loción
para el pelo.**
An eye cup, gauze, hair tonic.
aan ay cûp, goŝ, jer TAN-îc.

835. Una bolsa para agua caliente, un saquito para hielo.
A hot water bottle, an ice bag.
û jat HUOT-ûr BAT-ûl, aan ais baag.

836. Loción para picaduras, insecticida.
Insect bite lotion, insect repellent.
ÎN-sect bait LOU-shûn, ÎN-sect ri-PEL-ent.

837. Yodo, un laxante.
Iodine, a laxative.
AI- û-dain, û LAACS-î-tîv.

838. Lápiz de labios, un gotero.
Lipstick, a medicine dropper.
LÎP-stîc, û MED-î-sín DRAP-ûr.

839. Un gargarismo, agua oxigenada.
A mouth wash, peroxide.
û mauz huash, pûr-ACS-aid.

840. Veneno, polvos, quinina.
Poison, powder, quinine.
POI-ŝûn, PAU-dûr, CUAI-nain.

841. Colorete, servilletas higiénicas.
Rouge, sanitary napkins.
ruŝh, SAAN-î-ter-y NAAP-quînŝ.

842. Un sedante, (líquido, crema para) el champú.
A sedative, shampoo (liquid, cream).
û SED-û-tîv, shaam-PU (LÎC-uîd, crim).

843. Loción de afeitar, crema de afeitar (sin brocha).
Shaving lotion, (brushless) shaving cream.
SHEIV-îng LOU-shûn, (BRÛSH-lís) SHEIV-îng crim.

844. Jabón, ungüento para quemadura de sol, sales aromáticas.
Soap, sunburn ointment, smelling salts.
soup, SÛN-búrn OINT-ment, SMEL-îng solts.

845. Aceite de "sun tan," termómetro.
Sun tan oil, thermometer.
sûn taan oil, zûr-MAM-î-tûr.

846. (Pasta, polvos) para los dientes.
Tooth (paste, powder).
tuz (peist, PAU-dǔr).

847. Navaja de seguridad, hojas de afeitar.
Safety razor, razor blades.
SEIF-ti REI-ŝûr, REI-ŝûr bleidŝ.

PARTES DEL CUERPO
PARTS OF THE BODY

850. El tobillo. The ankle. *thi AAN-cûl.*

851. El apéndice. The appendix.
thi û-PEN-dîcs.

852. El brazo. The arm. *thi arm.*

853. La espalda. The back. *thû baac.*

854. La sangre. The blood. *thû blûd.*

855. El hueso. The bone. *thû boun.*

856. Le mejilla. The cheek. *thû chic.*

857. El pecho. The chest. *thû chest.*

858. La barba. The chin. *thû chîn.*

859. La clavícula. The collar bone.
thû CAL-ûr-boun.

860. La oreja. The ear. *thi ear.*

861. El codo. The elbow. *thi EL-bou.*

862. El ojo. The eye. *thi ay.*

863. Las cejas. The eyebrows.
thi AI-brauŝ.

864. Las pestañas. The eyelashes.
thi AI-laash-îŝ.

865. El párpado. The eyelid. *thi AI-lîd.*

866. La cara. The face. *thû feis.*

867. El dedo. The finger. *thû FÎNG-ûr.*

868. El pie. The foot. *thû fût.*

869. La frente. The forehead. *thû FOR-ed.*

870. El pelo. The hair. *thû jer.*

871. La mano. The hand. *thû jaand.*

872. La cabeza. The head. *thû jed.*

873. El corazón. The heart. *thû jart.*

874. El talón. The heel. *thû jil.*

875. La cadera. The hip. *thû jîp.*

876. Los intestinos. The intestines.
   thi ín-TES-tínŝ.

877. La mandíbula. The jaw. *thû dcho(r).*

878. La coyuntura. The joint.
   thû dchoint.

879. El riñón. The kidney. *thû QUÍD-ni.*

880. La rodilla. The knee. *thû ni.*

881. La pierna. The leg. *thû leg.*

882. El labio. The lip. *thû líp.*

883. El hígado. The liver. *thû LÍV-ûr.*

884. El pulmón. The lung. *thû lûng.*

885. La boca. The mouth. *thû mauz.*

886. El músculo. The muscle. *thû MÚS-ûl.*

887. La uña. The nail. *thû neil.*

888. El cuello. The neck. *thû nɛc.*

889. El nervio. The nerve. *thû nûrv.*

890. La nariz. The nose. *thû nouŝ.*

891. La costilla. The rib. *thû ríb.*

892. El hombro. The shoulder.
   thû SHOUL-dûr.

893. El costado (derecho, izquierdo).
   The (right, left) side.
   thû (rait, left) said.

894. El piel. The skin. *thû squîn.*

895. El cráneo. The skull. *thû scûl.*

896. La espina. The spine. *thû spain.*

897. El estómago. The stomach.
thû STÛM-úc.

898. El diente. The tooth. *thû tuz.*

899. El muslo. The thigh. *thû zay.*

900. La garganta. The throat. *thû zrout.*

901. El pulgar. The thumb. *thû zûm.*

902. El dedo del pie. The toe. *thû tou.*

903. La lengua. The tongue. *thû tûng.*

904. Las amígdalas. The tonsils.
thû TAN-sîlŝ.

905. La cintura. The waist. *thû hueist.*

906. La muñeca. The wrist. *thû rîst.*

COMUNICACIONES: TELÉFONO
COMMUNICATIONS: TELEPHONE

909. ¿Dónde puedo telefonear?
Where can I telephone?
huer caan ay TEL-û-foun?

910. ¿Quisiera telefonear de mi parte?
Will you please telephone for me?
hûil yu pliŝ TEL-û-foun for mi?

911. Deseo hacer una llamada a ——.
I want to make a local call to ——.
ay huant tu meic û LOU-cûl col tu ——.

912. Una llamada de larga distancia.
A long distance call.
û long DÍS-tûns col.

913. La telefonista le llamará.
The operator will call you.
thi AP-ûr-ei-tûr huíl col yu.

914. Quiero el número ——.
I want number ——.
ay huant NÛM-bûr ——.
Véase NÚMEROS, pág. 96.

915. Aló. Hello. *jel-OU.*

916. No contestan. They do not answer.
they du nat AAN-sûr.

917. La línea está ocupada.
The line is busy.
ihû lain ís BÍS-y.

918. ¿Puedo hablar con ——?
May I speak to ——?
mey ay spic tu ——?

919. Él no está. He is not in. *ji ís nat ín.*

920. Habla ——. This is —— speaking.
thís ís —— SPI-quíng.

921. Haga el favor de tomar un mensaje para ——.
Please take a message for ——.
plíş teic û MES-îdch for ——.

922. Mi número de teléfono es ——.
My number is ——.
may NÚM-búr ís ——.

923. ¿Cuánto cuesta llamar a ——?
How much is a call to ——?
jou múch ís û col tu ——?

924. Le llaman por teléfono.
There is a telephone call for you.
ther ís û TEL-û-foun col for yu.

TELEGRAMAS Y CABLEGRAMAS
TELEGRAMS AND CABLEGRAMS

927. ¿Dónde puedo poner un (telegrama, cablegrama)?
Where can I send a (telegram, cablegram)?
huer caan ay send û (TEL-û-graam, QUEI-búl-graam)?

928. ¿Cuánto por palabra a ——?
What is the rate per word to ——?
huat ís thú reit púr u-ÚRD tu ——?

929. ¿Dónde están las formas?
Where are the forms?
huer ar thú formś?

930. Quiero pagar la respuesta.
I wish to pay for the answer.
ay huísh tu pey for thi AAN-súr.

931. Urgente.   ¿Cuándo llegará?
Urgent.   When will it arrive?
ÚRD-chent.   huen huíl ít û-RAIV?

INFORMES ÚTILES
  DÍAS DE LA SEMANA
USEFUL INFORMATION
  DAYS OF THE WEEK

933. Domingo.   Sunday.   *SÛN-dey.*

934. Lunes, martes.
  Monday, Tuesday.
  MÛN-dey, TIUŜ-dey.

935. Miércoles, jueves.
  Wednesday, Thursday.
  HUENŜ-dey, ZÛRŜ-day.

936. Viernes, sábado.
  Friday, Saturday.
  FRAI-dey, SAAT-ûr-dey.

MESES, ESTACIONES Y TIEMPO
MONTHS, SEASONS AND WEATHER

939. Enero, febrero.
  January, February.
  DCHAAN-yu-er-y, FEB-ru-er-y.

940. Marzo, abril.
  March, April.
  march, HEI-príl.

941. Mayo, junio.
  May, June.
  mey, dchun.

942. Julio, agosto.
  July, August.
  dchu-LAY, OG-ûst.

943. Septiembre, octubre.
September, October.
sep-TEM-bûr, ac-TOU-bûr.

944. Noviembre, diciembre.
November, December.
nou-VEM-bûr, di-SEM-bûr.

945. La primavera, el verano.
Spring, Summer.
sprîng, SÛM-ûr.

946. El otoño, el invierno.
Fall, Winter.
fol, HUÎN-tûr.

947. Hace (calor, frío).
It is (warm, cold).
ît îŝ (huorm, could).

948. Hace (sol, buen tiempo, mal tiempo).
It is (fair, good, bad).
ît îŝ (feir, gûd, baad).

949. Está (lloviendo, nevando).
It is (raining, snowing).
ît îŝ (REIN-îng, SNOU-îng).

950. El ŝol, asoleado, la sombra.
The sun, sunny, the shade.
thû sûn, SÛN-y, thû sheid.

HORA, ETC.
TIME AND TIME EXPRESSIONS

953. ¿Qué hora es? What time is it?
huat taim îŝ ît?

954. Son las dos.
It is two o'clock.
ît îs̱ tu ou-CLAC.

955. Son las seis y media.
It is half past six.
ît îs̱ jaaf paast sîcs̱.

956. Son las ocho y cuarto.
It is a quarter past eight.
ît îs̱ û CUOR-tûr paast heit.

957. Son las nueve menos cuarto.
It is a quarter to nine.
ît îs̱ û CUOR-tûr tu nain.

958. A la(s) —— menos diez.
At ten minutes to ——.
aat ten MÎN-îts tu ——.

Véase NÚMEROS, pág. 96.

959. A la(s) —— y diez.
At ten minutes past ——.
aat ten MÎN-îts paast ——.

960. Por la mañana, por la noche.
In the morning, in the evening.
în thû MOR-nîng, în thi IV-nîng.

961. Por la tarde, a mediodía.
In the afternoon, at noon.
în thi aaf-tûr-NUN, aat nun.

962. El día, la noche, la medianoche.
Day, night, midnight.
dey, nait, MÎD-nait.

963. Ayer, anoche.
    Yesterday, last night.
    YES-tûr-dey, laast nait.

964. Hoy, esta noche, mañana.
    Today, tonight, tomorrow.
    tû-DEY, tû-NAIT, tû-MOR-ou.

965. Anteayer.
    (The) day before yesterday.
    (thû) dey bi-FOR YES-tûr-dey.

966. El año pasado, el mes pasado.
    Last year, last month.
    laast yir, laast mûnz.

967. El lunes que viene, la semana próxima.
    Next Monday, next week.
    necst MÛN-dey, necst huic.

968. Hace dos semanas.
    Two weeks ago.
    tu huics û-GOU.

NÚMEROS CARDINALES
CARDINAL NUMBERS

969.   1 **Uno.**   One.   *huon.*
       2 **Dos.**   Two.   *tu.*
       3 **Tres.**   Three.   *zri.*
       4 **Cuatro.**   Four.   *for.*
       5 **Cinco.**   Five.   *faiv.*
       6 **Seis.**   Six.   *sîcŝ.*
       7 **Siete.**   Seven.   *SEV-en.*
       8 **Ocho.**   Eight.   *heit.*

9 **Nueve** Nine. *nain.*

10 **Diez.** Ten. *ten.*

11 **Once.** Eleven. *i-LEV-en.*

12 **Doce.** Twelve. *tuelv.*

13 **Trece.** Thirteen. *ZÛR-tin.*

14 **Catorce.** Fourteen. *FOR-tin.*

15 **Quince.** Fifteen. *FÎF-tin.*

16 **Diez y seis.** Sixteen. *SÎCS-tin.*

17 **Diez y siete.** Seventeen. *SEV-en-tin.*

18 **Diez y ocho.** Eighteen. *HEI-tin.*

19 **Diez y nueve.** Nineteen. *NAIN-tin.*

20 **Veinte.** Twenty. *TUEN-ti.*

21 **Veinte y uno.** Twenty-one. *tuen-ti-HUON.*

22 **Veinte y dos.** Twenty-two. *tuen-ti-TU.*

30 **Treinta.** Thirty. *ZÛR-ti.*

31 **Treinta y uno.** Thirty-one. *zûr-ti-HUON.*

40 **Cuarenta**. Forty. *FOR-ti.*

50 **Cincuenta.** Fifty. *FÎF-ti.*

60 **Sesenta.** Sixty. *SÎCS-ti.*

70 **Setenta.** Seventy. *SEV-en-ti.*

80 **Ochenta.** Eighty. *HEI-ti.*

90 **Noventa.** Ninety. *NAIN-ti.*

100 **Cien.** One hundred. *huon JÛN-dred.*

101 **Ciento uno.** One hundred one. *huon JÛN-dred huon.*

102 **Ciento dos.** One hundred two. *huon JÛN-dred tu.*

110 **Ciento diez.** One hundred ten.
huon JÛN-dred ten.

120 **Ciento veinte.** One hundred twenty.
huon JÛN-dred TUEN-ti.

200 **Doscientos.** Two hundred.
tu JÛN-dred.

1,000 **Mil.** One thousand.
huon ZAU-sûnd.

1,001 **Mil uno.** One thousand one.
huon ZAU-sûnd huon.

2,000 **Dos mil.** Two thousand.
tu ZAU-sûnd.

100,000 **Cien mil.**
One hundred thousand.
huon JÛN-dred ZAU-sûnd.

1,000,000 **Un millón.**
One million.
huon MÎL-yûn.

NÚMEROS ORDINALES
ORDINAL NUMBERS

Primero. First. *fûrst.*
Segundo. Second. *SEC-ûnd.*
Tercero. Third. *zûrd.*
Cuarto. Fourth. *forz.*
Quinto. Fifth. *fîfz.*
Sexto. Sixth. *sîcsz.*
Séptimo. Seventh. *SEV-enz.*
Octavo. Eighth. *heiz.*
Noveno. Ninth. *nainz.*
Décimo. Tenth. *tenz.*

Vigésimo. Twentieth. *TUEN-ti-ez.*
Quincuagésimo. Fiftieth. *FÎF-ti-ez.*
Centésimo. Hundredth. *JÛN-dredz.*

MEDIDAS
MEASUREMENTS

970. ¿Qué largo (ancho) tiene?
What is the length (width)?
huat îŝ thû lengz (huîdz)?

971. ¿Cuánto por yarda?
How much is it per yard?
jau mûch îŝ ît pûr yard?

972. ¿De qué tamaño es?
What is the size?
huat îŝ thû saiŝ?

973. Tiene diez pies de largo por cuatro pies de ancho.
It is ten feet long by four feet wide.
ît îŝ ten fit long bay for fit huaid.

974. Alto, bajo. High, low. *jay, lou.*

975. Grande, pequeño, mediano.
Large, small, medium.
lardch, smol, MI-di-ûm.

976. Igual, diferente.
Alike, different.
û-LAIC, DÎF-ûŗ-ent.

977. Un par, una docena.
A pair, a dozen.
û per, û DÛŜ-en.

978. Media docena.
Half a dozen.
jaaf û DÛŜ-en.

979. Media yarda.
Half a yard.
jaaf û yard.

980. Es demasiado (estrecho, flojo).
It is too (tight, loose).
ît îŝ tu (tait, lus).

981. Ancho, angosto, largo, corto.
Wide, narrow, long, short.
huaid, NAAR-ou, long; short.

COLORES
COLORS

982. Claro, obscuro.
Light, dark.
lait, darc.

983. Negro, azul, moreno.
Black, blue, brown.
blaac, blu, braun.

984. Crema, gris, verde.
Cream, gray, green.
crim, grey, grin.

985. Anaranjado, rosado, morado.
Orange, pink, purple.
AR-endch, pínc, PÛR-púl.

986. Rojo, blanco, amarillo.
Red, white, yellow.
red, huait, ÝEL-ou.

987. Quiero un tono (más claro, obscuro).
I want a (lighter, darker) shade.
ay huant û (LAIT-ûr, DARC-ûr) sheid.

PALABRAS ÚTILES
USEFUL WORDS

991. Cenicero.   Ash tray.   *aash trey.*

992. Saco.   Bag.   *baag.*

993. Canasta.   Basket.   *BAAS-quît.*

994. Horquillas.   Bobby pins.   *BAB-y pînŝ.*

995. Caja.   Box.   *bacs.*

996. Pulsera.   Bracelet.   *BREIS-lît.*

997. Bombilla.   Bulb.   *búlb.*

998. Botón.   Button.   *BÛT-ún.*

999. Lata   Tin (can).   *(tín) caan.*

1000. Dulces.   Candy.   *CAAN-di.*

1001. Abrelatas.   Can opener.
caan OU-pen-ûr.

1002. Taquilla de cambio.   Change booth.
cheindch buz.

1003. Pedicuro.   Chiropodist.   *cû-RAP-û-dîst.*

1004. Certificado de ciudadanía.
   Citizenship papers.
   CÍT-iŝ-en-ŝhîp PEIP-ûrŝ.

1005. Clínica (médica).
   (Medical) Clinic.
   (MED-î-cûl) CLÍN-îc.

1006. Clínica (dental).
   (Dental) Clinic.
   (DEN-tûl) CLÍN-îc.

1007. Horquillas de tender.
   Clothespins.
   CLOUŜ-pînŝ.

1008. Botón de cuello.
   Collar button.
   CAL-ûr BÛT-ûn.

1009. Tapón.   Cork.   *corc.*

1010. Tirabuzón.   Corkscrew.   *CORC-scru.*

1011. Algodón.   Cotton.   *CAT-ûn.*

1012. Ramillete.   Corsage.   *cor-SADCH.*

1013. Crédito.   Credit.   *CRED-ît.*

1014. Gemelos.   Cuff links.   *CÛF lìncs.*

1015. Cortina.   Curtain.   *CÛR-tîn.*

1016. Cojín.   Cushion.   *CÛSH-în.*

1017. Almacén. Department store.
dú-PART-ment stor.

1018. Arete. Earring. *IR-îng.*

1019. Elevado. Elevated train.
EL-î-veit-ed trein.

1020. Ventilador. Fan. *faan.*

1021. Botiquín. First-aid kit.
fûrst-HEID quît.

1022. Linterna eléctrica. Flashlight.
FLAASH-lait.

1023. Flores. Flowers. *FLAU-ûrŝ.*

1024. Lentes. Glasses (eyeglasses).
GLAAS-îŝ (AI-glass-îŝ).

1025. Oro. Gold. *gould.*

1026. Chicle. (Chewing) gum.
(CHU-îng) gûm.

1027. Redecilla. Hairnet. *JER-net.*

1028. Horquilla. Hairpin. *JER-pîn.*

1029. Bolsa. Handbag. *JAAND-baag.*

1030. Pañuelo. Handkerchief.
JAAN-cûr-chîf.

1031. Certificado de sanidad.
Health certificate.
jelz sûr-TÍF-î-cût.

1032. Tacón. Heel. *jil.*

1033. Ganchito. Hook. *júc.*

1034. Casilla de información.
Information booth.
in-for-MEI-shún buz.

1035. Seguro (sobre el auto).
(Automobile) insurance.
(OT-o-mo-bil) in-SHUR-úns.

1036. Seguro (sobre la vida).
(Life) insurance.
(laif) in-SHUR-úns.

1037. Seguro (para viajeros).
(Travel) insurance.
(TRAAV-úl) in-SHUR-úns.

1038. Plancha. Iron. *AI-úrn.*

1039. Etiqueta. Label. *LEI-búl.*

1040. Encaje. Lace (for trimming).
leis (for TRÎM-íng).

1041. Cinta (de zapatos).
Lace (for shoes).
leis (for shuś).

1042. Bibloteca (pública).
(Public) library.
(PÚB-líc) LAI-brer-y.

1043. Lino. Linen. *LÎN-en.*

1044. Mosquitero.   Mosquito net.
mûs-QUI-tou net.

1045. Clavo.   Nail.   *neil.*

1046. Lima de uñas.   Nail file.   *neil fail.*

1047. Aguja.   Needle.   *NI-dûl.*

1048. Libreta.   Notebook.   *NOUT-búc.*

1049. Nylon.   Nylon.   *NAI-lan.*

1050. Oculista.   Oculist.   *AC-yû-lîst.*

1051. Oficina.   Office.   *OF-îs.*

1052. Dueño.   Owner.   *OUN-ûr.*

1053. Candado.   Padlock.   *PAAD-lac.*

1054. Cubo.   Pail.   *peil.*

1055. Cortaplumas.   Penknife.   *PEN-naif.*

1056. Perfume.   Perfume.   *PÛRF-yum.*

1057. Broche.   (Ornamental) pin.
(or-na-MEN-tûl) pîn.

1058. Alfiler.   (Straight) pin.   *(streit) pîn.*

1059. Vasijas de barro.   Pottery.
PAT-ûr-y.

1060. Borla de polvos.   Powder puff.
PAU-dûr púf.

1061. Pregunta.   Question.   *CUES-chûn.*

1062. Rayón.   Rayon.   *REI-an.*

1063. Recibo.   Receipt.   *ri-SIT.*

1064. Religión.   Religion.   *rû-LÎD-chûn.*

1065. Anillo.   Ring.   *rîng.*

1066. Chanclos.   Rubbers.   *RÛB-ûrŝ.*

1067. Imperdible.   Safety pin.   *SEIF-ti pîn.*

1068. Tijeras.   Scissors.   *SÎS-ûrŝ.*

1069. Gancho.   Screw hook.   *scru jûc.*

1070. Betún.   Shoe polish.   *shu PAL-îsh.*

1071. Ducha.   Shower.   *SHAU-ûr.*

1072. Seda.   Silk.   *sîlc.*

1073. Plata.   Silver.   *SÎL-vûr.*

1074. Jabón en escamas.   Soap flakes.
soup fleics.

1075. Piedra (preciosa).   (Precious) stone.
(PRESH-ûs) stoun.

1076. Tapón.   Stopper.   *STAP-ûr.*

1077. Correa.   Strap.   *straap.*

1078. Paja.   Straw.   *stro(r).*

1079. Subterráneo.   Subway.   *SÛB-huey.*

1080. Lentes ahumados.   Sun glasses.
sûn GLAAS-îŝ.

1081. **Esparadrapo.** (Adhesive) tape. *(aad-JI-sív) teip*.

1082. **Cinta de envolver.** (Wrapping) tape. *(RAAP-íng) teip*.

1083. **Dedal.** Thimble. *ZÍM-búl*.

1084. **Hilo.** Thread. *zred*.

1085. **Ficha.** Token. *TOU-quen*.

1086. **Juguete.** Toy. *toy*.

1087. **Transbordo.** Transfer. *TRAANS-fûr*.

1088. **Cuerda o cordón.** Twine. *tuain*.

1089. **Máquina de escribir.** Typewriter. *TAIP-rait-úr*.

1090. **Paraguas.** Umbrella. *ûm-BREL-û*.

1091. **Vacaciones.** Vacation. *vei-QUEI-shûn*.

1092. **Termos.** Vacuum bottle. *VAAC-yûm BAT-úl*.

1093. **Florero.** Vase. *veis*.

1094. **Máquina de vender.** Vending machine. *VEND-íng mû-SHIN*.

1095. **Cartera.** Wallet. *HUAL-ít*.

1096. Trapo.   Wash cloth.   *HUASH-cloz.*

1097. Reloj (de pulsera).   (Wrist) watch.
(*ríst*) *huach.*

1098. Escobilla.   Whiskbroom.
HUÎSC-brum.

1099. Alambre.   Wire.   *HUAI-ûr.*

1100. Madera.   Wood.   *U-ûd.*

1101. Lana.   Wool.   *U-úl.*

1102. Cierre de cremallera.   Zipper.
ŜÎP-ûr.

ÍNDICE